· December 2001·

Margaret

Merry C[...]

Wonderful [...] year!

Remember you can always
call me with any cooking
questions ???

Love you,

Christine and
Julia

NOODLES & RICE

THE FOOD LOVER'S GUIDE
TO NOODLES AND RICE

NOODLES & RICE

THE FOOD LOVER'S GUIDE TO NOODLES AND RICE

THUNDER BAY
P·R·E·S·S

Published in the United States by
Thunder Bay Press,
An imprint of the Advantage Publishers Group
5880 Oberlin Drive
San Diego, CA 92121-4794
www.advantagebooksonline.com

All notations of errors or omissions should be addressed to Thunder Bay Press, editorial department, at the above address. All other correspondence (author inquiries, permissions and rights) concerning the content of this book should be addressed to Quantum Books, London

QUMBCND

ISBN 1-57145-235-4

Library of Congress Cataloging-in-Publication Data available upon request.

1 2 3 4 5 00 01 02 03 04

This book is produced by
Quantum Books
The Old Brewery, 6 Blundell Street
London N7 9BH

Designer: Bruce Low
Editor: Sarah King

This book was compiled using material from:
The Noodles Cookbook, Complete Chinese Cooking, Vietnamese Cooking, The Rice Cookbook, Classic Rice Dishes and Thai Cooking.

Manufactured in Singapore by Pica Graphics
Printed in Singapore by Star Standard Industries Pte. Ltd.

Contents

····

INTRODUCTION

Noodles and Rice brings you a wide variety of delicious ways of serving up two staples of the Asian diet which have become firmly established in Western cuisine - noodles and rice.

The book is divided into seven sections: Soups; Stir-Fried Noodles; Vegetables and Rice; Cold Noodle Dishes; Meat and Rice; Noodles with Toppings; and Desserts.

Although meat is used in many of the recipes, it is often in relatively small quantities within a dish and a vegetarian could quite easily adapt many of the recipes to exclude the meat element and still produce a complete meal. Many of the recipes use tofu which is high in protein and a healthy and nutritious alternative to meat. Prawns are also widely used and with their firm juicy texture make a fine complement to vegetable dishes with rice or noodles.

Recipes for basic soups and stocks are to be found in the Soup chapter and these feature in many of the later recipes. It is possible to make large batches of stock and freeze them. Before freezing, cool thoroughly and remove excess fat.

The Stir-Fried Noodles chapter shows you how to prepare tasty noodle dishes very quickly, mostly with the use of your wok, while the Vegetable and Rice chapter shows several different ways of serving up rice, including the very exotic Pineapple and Rice which is served out in a hollowed-out pineapple - very easy to make but a most impressive-looking dish to put before your guests.

The Cold Noodle Dishes are particularly easy to prepare because you don't have to worry about keeping parts of the dish hot while you prepare the rest.

The Meat and Rice chapter has recipes for a whole range of meats - chicken, beef, lamb, pork - some very quick, such as the Savoury Sausage and Bacon Kebabs in Tomato Sauce, and others more elaborate such as Crown Roast of Lamb with Apricot Rice Stuffing. There are also some delicious sauces to bring out the full flavour of the meat, such as saté sauce, made from peanut butter and soya chilli sauce. The marinades, popular in Asian cooking, can make the most exquisitely flavoursome dish out of a very ordinary steak or chop.

Some recipes in the Noodles with Toppings section involve deep-frying the noodles in basket shapes in which you then serve the remaining ingredients. These make a very attractive way of serving noodles for more special occasions.

Finally, in the Desserts chapter, there are some delicious and wholesome desserts using rice and fruit such as the very

using rice and fruit such as the very unusual sounding Rice Eggs with Peach Sauce or the more conventional Rice Soufflé Pudding.

Most of the ingredients recommended in these recipes can easily be found in the supermarket - others you may have to search out in a specialist food shop. Here are some of the ingredients that feature in many of the recipes and which are typical ingredients of rice and noodle dishes:

Beansprouts - very nutritious and crunchy, they are the sprouts of the green mung bean. They do not keep for long and need to be consumed while they are still fresh.

Beancurd or tofu - high in protein and popular as a meat substitute, tofu has a rather bland taste but has a pleasant texture and can be made very tasty with the right sauces. It is made from soya beans and sold in some supermarkets and most healthfood shops. Tofu should be cooked carefully as overhandling can cause the chunks to disintegrate.

Lemongrass - sold either dried or fresh, lemon grass adds a lovely perfume and taste to the dish. The dried version is really only suitable for herbal tea, and it is the fresh version that you want for adding to recipes. Use within about a week of purchase and store in the refrigerator.

Mirin - a sweet Japanese cooking wine which adds sweetness to sauces and complements grilled dishes.

Light Soy Sauce - full of flavor and more salty than dark soy sauce and therefore more suitable for adding to cooking.

Dark Soy Sauce - thicker and stronger than light soy sauce, this is used in some recipes (often a combination of the two is required). Dark soy sauce is more suitable than the light sort for adding flavor to a dish at the table.

Miso Paste - made from fermented soya beans and barley or rice malt, used to add flavor to a dish.

OVEN TEMPERATURES GUIDE		
C	F	Gas Mark
240	475	9
230	450	8
220	425	7
200	400	6
190	375	5
180	350	4
165	325	3
150	300	2
140	275	1
125	250	$1/2$
110	225	$1/4$

Chapter One

Soups

A selection of delicious soups and broths. Many can either be eaten as a wholesome soup or form the basic ingredient of a main dish.

INGREDIENTS

560 g/1¼ lb chicken bones (such as carcasses, wings, feet etc.), chopped roughly
110 g/4 oz pork bones
1 small onion, cut in half
20 cm/8 in leek, cut in half diagonally
2 fat cloves garlic, minced
2.5 cm/1 in fresh ginger, peeled and sliced
10 cups/2.25 l/4 pt water

INGREDIENTS

7½ cups/1.75 l/3 pt water
3 chicken drumsticks

INGREDIENTS

2 Tbsp *mirin*
6¼ cups1.5 l/2½ pt premier *dashi*
½ cup/90 ml/3½ floz Japanese soy sauce
3 Tbsp superfine sugar

CHICKEN BROTH
MAKES 1.75 l/7½ CUPS

Used to make Chinese and Ramen hot noodle soups and Chinese sauces. Pork bones can be replaced with more chicken bones if wished.

Wash the bones before use. Blanch the chicken and pork bones in boiling water for 2 minutes. Rinse.

Put the bones, onion, leek, garlic, ginger and water in a large pan. Bring to aboil, then simmer for 1 hour, skimming off the scum occasionally. After an hour, strain the broth through a very fine mesh strainer or muslin.

LIGHT CHICKEN BROTH
MAKES 1.5 l/6 CUPS

Put the water and chicken drumsticks in a saucepan, bring to a boil and simmer for about 40 minutes. When the meat on the drumstick shin begins to fall away, exposing the bone, the broth should be ready. Strain through a metal sieve and reserve the drumstick meat as a topping for a noodle dish.

DASHI SAUCE
MAKES 1.5 l /6 CUPS

Put the *mirin* in a saucepan and bring to a boil. Add the *dashi*, soy sauce and sugar and simmer for about 3–4 minutes. It is now ready to use.

SOY SAUCE BROTH

MAKES 1.5 1/6 CUPS

Put the broth, salt, wine and lard in a pan. Bring to a boil and simmer for 2–3 minutes. Turn off the heat and add the light and dark soy sauce, black pepper and stir. It is now ready to use.

INGREDIENTS

6 cups/1.5 1/2½ pt chicken broth

2 tsp salt

4 tsp Chinese rice wine or Japanese *sake*

10 g/½ oz lard

4 Tbsp light soy sauce

4 tsp dark soy sauce

black pepper

PREMIER JAPANESE DASHI

MAKES 1.5 1/6 CUPS

INGREDIENTS

6 cups/1.5 1/2½ pt water

4-inch piece dried kelp (konbu), wiped with a damp cloth

3 cups/12 oz bonito flakes (katsuo-bushi)

Used for making Japanese broth.

First, make two or three cuts about 1 in long in the kelp to release more flavour, then put the water and kelp in a saucepan and heat under a low flame. Remove the kelp just before the water begins to boil.

Add the bonito flakes when the liquid comes back to a boil, and turn off the heat. Leave the liquid until the flakes sink to the bottom of the pan, then strain through a muslin or paper filter. Retain the bonito flakes and kelp for preparing standard *dashi*.

MISO SAUCE

MAKES 1.5 1/6 CUPS

Heat the oil in a pan. Add the ginger, garlic and scallion and fry for 30 seconds. Add the wine first, then soy sauce, sugar, *miso* paste and chili oil and mix together. Add the chicken broth and bring to the boil. Remove from the heat and the sauce is now ready to use.

INGREDIENTS

1 Tbsp sesame oil

1 cm/½ in fresh ginger, peeled and minced

1 fat clove garlic, minced

1 scallion, minced

4 Tbsp Chinese rice wine or Japanese *sake*

3 Tbsp light soy sauce

2 Tbsp superfine sugar

8 Tbsp red *miso* paste

2 tsp chili oil

6 cups/1.5 1/2½ pt chicken broth

black pepper

INGREDIENTS

1 Tbsp vegetable oil
1 fat *clove garlic, sliced*
2.5 cm/1 in fresh ginger, sliced
½ leek, sliced
50 g/2 oz carrots, chopped
1 medium-sized onion, chopped
1½ sticks celery, chopped
2 cups/1.1/2 pt water

VEGETABLE BROTH
MAKES ABOUT 4 ½ CUPS/1 L

For vegetarians, vegetable broth can be substituted for chicken broth.

Heat the oil in a saucepan and fry all the vegetables for 2 minutes. Add the water, bring to a boil and simmer for 40 minutes. Strain through a metal strainer.

INGREDIENTS

2½ cups/1.5 l/2½ pt water
used kelp and bonito flakes from premier *dashi*

STANDARD JAPANESE DASHI
MAKES ABOUT 6 ½ CUPS/1.5 L

Standard dashi recycles bonito flakes and kelp used to make Premier Japanese Dashi. It is used in the same way.

Put the water, kelp and bonito flakes in a large saucepan. Bring to a boil over a low heat and simmer for about 5 minutes. Skim off any scum that forms on the surface. Sieve through muslin or a coffee filter.

Dipping Sauce
MAKES ABOUT 1 1/4 CUPS / 725 ml

INGREDIENTS

¾ cup/175 ml/6 floz *mirin*

2¼ cup/500 ml/18 floz spremier *dashi*

¾ cup/175 ml/6 floz Japanese soy sauce

Put the *mirin* in a saucepan and bring to a boil. Add the *dashi* and soy sauce and simmer for 3–4 minutes, then remove from the heat and chill in the refrigerator
.

Dipping sauce can be stored refrigerated in a jar for 3–4 days.

Making Fresh Udon

INGREDIENTS

2 Tbsp salt

1 cup/200 ml/7 floz water

1½ cup/175 g/6 oz strong flour

2 cups/250 g/9 oz all-purpose flour

all-purpose flour for dusting

Making udon noodles is usually a professional job in Japan, and both fresh and dried udon are widely available in the stores. A key point to successful home-made udon is good, hard kneading. If you cannot bring yourself to use your feet and tread on the dough, you can knead by hand. Just make sure you knead well. When you knead the dough with your feet, remember to take off your shoes! Fresh Udon can be refrigerated in a plastic bag for up to three days.

Dissolve the salt in the water in a cup. Sift the strong and all-purpose flours together into a large bowl. Add the salted water little by little, mixing with chopsticks or a fork, Then, with your fingers, mix to a breadcrumb consistency.

Knead with your hands and then form the dough into a round. Wrap with a wet cloth and leave for 30–60 minutes. Dust your worktop with flour, knead again, shape into a round and put into a strong plastic bag. Using your feet knead the dough for 10 minutes.

Remove the dough from the bag. Dust the worktop with flour and roll the dough out to a thickness of ¼ in/5 mm. Dust with flour again, then fold the dough, so you can slice it easily into ¼ in/5 mm strips.

INGREDIENTS

4 pork chops, off the bone and lightly
tenderized

6½ cups/1.5 l /2½ pt chicken broth

1 tbsp Chinese rice wine or dry sherry

2 tsp salt

white pepper

2 lettuce leaves, quartered

4–5 Tbsp vegetable oil

450 g/1 lb ramen noodles, or 400 g/14 oz
fresh or 300 g/11 oz dried medium egg
noodles

For the Marinade

1 clove garlic, minced

1 scallion, chopped

1 Tbsp light soy sauce

1 Tbsp dark soy sauce

2 Tbsp Chinese rice wine or dry sherry

1 Tbsp superfine sugar

a pinch of pepper

2 tsp cornstarch

EGG NOODLE SOUP WITH PORK CHOP

You would be hard pressed to find a better way of serving pork chops than with the fiery, sweet marinade used here. Strictly speaking, Chinese rice wine should be used in this dish but I have found that a dry sherry can be used as a substitute without any drastic change in flavor.

Mix the garlic, scallion, soy sauce, rice wine, sugar, pepper and cornstarch together, then marinate the pork chops for 30 minutes.

Meanwhile, put the chicken broth, rice wine, salt and pepper in a pan. Bring to a boil and simmer for 3 minutes. Blanch the lettuce leaves in a pan for 1 minute. Set aside.

Heat the oil in a wok or skillet. Shallow fry the pork chops for 2–3 minutes on each side until lightly browned. (Frying time will vary with the thickness of the pork.) Cut into strips 1 in wide.

Bring plenty of water to a boil in a large pan and add the egg noodles. Cook for 4 minutes or according to the instructions on the packet. Drain well and put into four bowls.

Place the pork and lettuce leaves on the noodles and pour the hot broth over. Serve immediately.

RAMEN WITH CRAB OMELET

INGREDIENTS

1 cup/450 g/1 lb *ramen* noodles, *or* 400 g/14
oz fresh *or* 300 g/11 oz dried thin egg
noodles
6¼ cups/1.5 l/2½ pt soy sauce broth

For the omelette
6 eggs
175 g/6 oz crab meat (canned)
4 *shiitake* mushrooms, sliced
2 scallions, thinly sliced
4 Tbsp canned bamboo shoots, thinly sliced
salt and white pepper
2–3 Tbsp vegetable oil
1 scallion, chopped

Typically, crab omelet is served on its own. The inspiration behind the dish is Chinese but the Japanese have a preference for it served on a bowl of noodles. Ideally, individual omelets for each person should be made, but if time is against you, make one large one and cut it into four.

First, to make the omelet, put the eggs, crab meat, mushrooms, scallions and bamboo shoots in a bowl. Season with salt and pepper, and mix.

Heat the oil in a skillet or wok until very hot. Pour in the egg mixture and heat for 30 seconds. Stir lightly with chopsticks or a spatula a few times. When it is nearly set, turn it over. The mixture should be soft like scrambled egg, but be cooked just enough to be able to retain the shape of an omelet.

Boil plenty of water in a large pan. Add the noodles and cook for 3 minutes, or according to the instruction on the packet. Drain and divide into four bowls.

Heat the soy sauce broth. Place the crab omelet on the noodles, and pour the broth over the top. Sprinkle with the chopped scallion and serve.

Udon with Bean Curd Sheet

Abura-age *are deep-fried sheets of tofu, available at most stores which broth Japanese foodstuffs. They can be stored at home in the freezer but will quickly go off if left for any time in the refrigerator.*

Rinse the *abura-age* in hot water. Put it into a saucepan of boiling water together with the *dashi*, sugar and soy sauce. Simmer for about 20 minutes or until the fluid has reduced to a third.

Bring plenty of water to boil in a pan and add the *udon*. Cook for 3 minutes.

Drain and rinse with cold water, then drain once more. Divide and put into individual serving bowls.

Blanch the spinach in boiling water for 1 minute, then drain and squeeze out the excess water. Heat the *dashi* sauce.

Put two half sheets of *abura-age*, some spinach and scallions onto each serving of *udon*. Pour the sauce over the top, sprinkle with the seven flavors chili powder and serve.

Ingredients

560 g/1¼ lb parboiled fresh *udon*

6½ cups/1.5 l /2½ pt *dashi* sauce

4 bean curd sheets (*abura-age*), cut into halves

1 cup/200 ml/7 floz premier *dashi*

2 Tbsp superfine sugar

2½ Tbsp soy sauce

220 g/8 oz fresh spinach

2 scallions, chopped

a pinch of salt

seven flavors chili powder (*shichimi*) (optional)

HOT NOODLE SOUP WITH SHRIMPS

Tam yam goong is one of the representative dishes of Thai cuisine. The soup is a myriad of flavors; the sour element of lime leaves and lemon grass combined with the hot chili pepper and nam pla with its strong seafood aroma.

Heat the oil in a saucepan, stir-fry the garlic, shallots, *galangal* and chili for about 1 minute. Put in the chicken broth, add the lime leaves and lemon grass, bring to a boil and simmer for 5 minutes.

Meanwhile, soak the rice vermicelli for 3 minutes, rinse, drain and divide into four bowls. Add the shrimps, fish sauce, lemon or lime juice, sugar and straw mushrooms to the soup and simmer for 2–3 minutes.

Pour the soup into the bowls and sprinkle with the cilantro leaves. Serve immediately.

INGREDIENTS

1 Tbsp vegetable oil
2 cloves garlic, shredded
2 shallots, shredded
2.5 cm/1 in *galangal* or ½-inch fresh ginger, thinly sliced
4–5 small red chilies, chopped
6½ cups/1.5 l /2½ pt light chicken broth
3 Kaffir lime leaves, sliced
10 cm/4 in lemon grass, chopped
2 cups/220 g/8 oz rice vermicelli
20 peeled tiger shrimps
6 Tbsp fish sauce (*nam pla*)
6 Tbsp fresh lemon or lime juice
2 Tbsp palm or brown sugar
16 canned straw mushrooms
cilantro leaves

23

UDON WITH CURRY SAUCE

A modern Japanese innovation combining the spicy flavor of a curry sauce with the smooth texture of udon *noodles.*

Heat the oil in a pan. Fry the chicken for 5 minutes or until cooked through. Set aside.

Add the onion and fry until lightly browned. Add the flour and curry powder and fry for 1–2 minutes.

Gradually dissolve the chicken bouillon into the water, add the chutney and currants and season with salt and pepper. Simmer for 10 minutes, then stir in the cooked chicken.

Bring plenty of water to a boil in a pan and add the *udon*. Cook for 3 minutes and drain. Rinse under cold water and drain again. Divide into serving bowls.

Meanwhile, heat the dashi sauce. Pour the curry sauce over the *udon* and pour the dashi sauce over the top. Serve immediately.

INGREDIENTS

560 g/1¼ lb parboiled fresh udon
6¼ cups/1.5 l/2½ pt *dashi* sauce

For the Curry

2 Tbsp vegetable oil
2 boneless chicken breasts, diced
1 medium-sized onion, sliced
2 Tbsp all-purpose flour
1–2 tsp curry powder
½ chicken bouillon cube
1¼ cup/300 ml/11 floz water
2 Tbsp chutney
½ cup/50 g/2 oz currants
salt and pepper

Miso Ramen with Shredded Leek

Noodles in miso *sauce are one of the most popular noodle dishes served in Japan. It is essential to use a good quality* miso *paste as this provides the crucial sweet and sour flavoring to the dish. The shredded leek should have a firm, supple texture, so if prepared beforehand, soak in a little water to prevent it from drying out.*

Bring some water to a boil in a pan and blanch the spinach for 1–2 minutes. Rinse, drain and divide into four equal portions. Bring more water to a boil in a large saucepan. Add the noodles and boil for 4 minutes. Drain and place into individual serving bowls.

Heat the *miso* sauce for 2–3 minutes. Pile the leek, spinach and bamboo shoots on top of the noodles. Add the *miso* sauce. Serve immediately.

Ingredients

1 cup/220 g/8 oz fresh spinach

1¾ cups/450 g/1 lb *ramen* noodles, *or* 400 g/14 oz fresh *or* 11 oz dried egg noodles

6¼ cups/1.5 l/2½ pt *miso* broth

10 cm/4 in leek, cut into four pieces and shredded

4 Tbsp cooked dried bamboo shoots (*shinachiku*) (optional)

Ingredients

1½ cups/400 g/14 oz dried *soba*
6¼ cups/1.5 l/2½ pt *dashi* sauce

For the Topping

3 boneless chicken breasts, sliced on a slant
into bite-sized pieces
2 Tbsp Japanese soy sauce
1 leek, thinly sliced diagonally
seven flavors chili powder (*shichimi*)
(optional)
cress for garnish

Soba with Chicken

The chicken used in this dish should be marinated for as long as possible to extract as much flavor from the sauce as possible, so don't be tempted to cut down on the times below, which should be treated as a minimum.

Marinate the chicken in the soy sauce for at least 15 minutes. Put the chicken, leek and *dashi* sauce in a saucepan, bring to a boil and simmer for 10–15 minutes or until the chicken is cooked. Occasionally skim off the scum.

Boil plenty of water in a large pan and add the *soba*. Cook for 5–6 minutes. Rinse well and drain thoroughly. Divide the *soba* into four bowls.

Pour the sauce with chicken and leek into the bowls. Garnish with the cress. Sprinkle with *shichimi* and serve at once.

RAMEN WITH BARBECUED PORK

Cha siu *is a spicy Chinese marinade and cha siu pork is widely eaten all over south-east Asia. Cha siu pork is roasted for a comparatively short time compared to roast pork dishes prepared in the West. Cha siu sauce is available from Chinese stores and bigger supermarkets.*

Boil plenty of water in a pan and cook the noodles for 3 minutes. Drain and divide into four bowls. Heat the soy sauce broth.

Put three slices of *cha siu* into each bowl of noodles. Garnish with the bamboo shoots and scallions. Pour the soy sauce broth over just before serving.

INGREDIENTS

2 cups/450 g/1 lb *ramen* noodles, *or* 14 oz fresh *or* 300 g/11 oz dried thin egg noodles
6¼ cups/1.5 l/2½ pt soy sauce broth

For the Topping

12 large slices Chinese style barbecued pork (*cha siu*)
4 Tbsp cooked dried bamboo shoots (*shinachiku*) (optional)
3 scallions, chopped

31

MISO UDON HOT POT

If you use dried udon, *boil it* al dente *first. You can leave out the chicken and make vegetarian hot pot, if you wish. Goba, a fibrous root vegetable, is available from Japanese stores.*

Put the *dashi*, chicken, carrots, rutabaga and leek in a saucepan, bring to a boil, and then add the *sake*, mushrooms and *goba* (if using). Simmer for 10–12 minutes.

Add the *udon* and cook for 3 minutes. Stir in the *miso* paste. When it comes back to a boil, it is ready to serve.

INGREDIENTS

7¼ cups/1.75 l/3 pt premier *dashi*

220 g/8 oz boneless chicken breasts, diced

75 g/3 oz carrots, sliced

175 g/6 oz rutabaga, sliced into bite-sized pieces

½ leek, sliced diagonally

2 Tbsp Japanese rice wine (*sake*)

50 g/2 oz *shimeji* mushrooms *or* 8 *shiitake* mushrooms

25 g/1 oz gobo (optional) thinly sliced

2 cups/450 g/1 lb parboiled fresh *udon*, rinsed

8 Tbsp *miso* paste

Vegetarian Noodles in Soup

Drain the ingredients if they are canned and cut the water chestnuts into thin slices. The straw mushrooms and white nuts can be left whole.

Heat the oil in a hot wok or skillet. When it starts to smoke, add the vegetables and stir-fry for a few seconds. Add the salt, sugar and soy sauce and continue stirring. When the gravy begins to boil, reduce the heat and let it simmer gently.

Cook the noodles in boiling water. Drain and place them in a large serving bowl. Pour a little of the water in which the noodles were cooked into the bowl – just enough to half-cover the noodles. Then quickly pour the entire contents of the wok or skillet over the top. Garnish with the sesame seed oil and serve hot.

Ingredients

1 cup/110 g/4 oz water chestnuts

220 g/8 oz straw mushrooms

1 cup/110 g/4 oz white nuts

3 Tbsp oil

1 tsp salt

1 tsp sugar

1 Tbsp light soy sauce

1 tsp sesame seed oil

1 cup/220 g/8 oz egg noodles or vermicelli

INGREDIENTS

2 cups/560 g/1¼ lb parboiled fresh *udon*

6¼ cups/1.5 l/2½ pt *dashi* sauce

For the Topping

4 *shiitake* mushrooms

1¼ cups/300 ml/11 floz *dashi*

2½ Tbsp soy sauce

2½ Tbsp *mirin*

220 g/8 oz fresh spinach

4 slices Japanese fishcake (*kamaboko*) or

seafood sticks

generous handful alfalfa sprouts

For the Omelettes

2 eggs

2 tsp *mirin*

¼ tsp soy sauce

a pinch of salt

2 tsp vegetable oil

UDON WITH FIVE TOPPINGS

A filling dish of udon *with several toppings. To make the Japanese-style omelet successfully a non-stick pan is essential. If you can't find a shop that stocks Japanese fish cake, or* kamabaka, *seafood sticks can be pressed into service in their place.*

Put the *shiitake*, *dashi*, soy sauce and *mirin* into a saucepan, bring to a boil and simmer for 8–10 minutes before setting aside. Discard the liquid when the *shiitake* are ready to be added to the *udon*.

To make the egg omelet, beat the eggs, *mirin*, soy sauce and salt together in a bowl. Heat the oil in a skillet. Pour a third of the egg mixture into the pan. When it is half set, gently roll it up and over to one side of the pan. Add another third of the mixture. Wait until this has half set, roll the first third over to the other side of the pan so it picks up the second third as it goes. Repeat once more before leaving to cool. When cooled, cut into eight pieces.

Cook the spinach in boiling water for 1–2 minutes. Rinse with cold water and squeeze out. Cut into four portions.

Cook the *udon* in a saucepan of boiling water for about 3 minutes. Rinse, drain and divide equally into four bowls.

Heat the *dashi* sauce. Put one *shiitake* mushroom, 2 slices of omelet, 1 portion of spinach, 1 slice of fish cake and a quarter of the cress into each bowl. Pour the hot *dashi* sauce over the top and serve immediately.

RAMEN WITH STIR-FRIED VEGETABLES

INGREDIENTS

2 cups/450 g/1 lb *ramen* noodles, *or* 14 oz
fresh *or* 300 g/11 oz dried thin egg noodles
6¼ cups/1.5 l/2½ pt soy sauce broth

For the Topping

2 Tbsp vegetable oil
1 Tbsp sesame oil
1 small onion, sliced
75 g/3 oz mangetout, cut in half diagonally
50 g/2 oz carrots, cut into long matchsticks
1 cup/200 g/7 oz bean sprouts
1 cup/200 g/7 oz Chinese leaves, chopped
2 dried black ear fungi or dried *shiitakie*
mushrooms, soaked in water, rinsed and
chopped
salt and pepper

Ramen *noodles topped with a blend of fresh and flash-fried vegetables – deliciously simple and simply delicious!*

Heat the oils in a wok or skillet until very hot. Stir-fry the onion, snow peas and carrots for 2 minutes, then add the bean sprouts, Chinese leaves, black fungi and stir-fry for another 3–4 minutes. Season with salt and pepper.

Boil plenty of water in a large pan and add the noodles. Cook for 3 minutes before draining well. Put the noodles into four bowls.

Heat the soy sauce broth. Pile the stir-fried vegetables onto the noodles and pour the broth over. Serve at once.

CREAMY COCONUT NOODLE SOUP

A famous Malaysian dish reflecting the multi-cultural nature of that country and its people. Laksa lemak should be treated with caution. Eat it once and you will be hopelessly addicted to its smooth texture and silky hot taste!

Blend the shallots, garlic, *galangal*, red chili and lemon grass in a mixer or food processor. Heat 3 tablespoons of the oil in a saucepan and stir-fry the shallot mixture with the turmeric, coriander and dried shrimp paste over a low heat for 3–4 minutes.

Heat the remaining oil in a skillet and fry the bean curd until lightly browned.

Add the chicken broth, coconut milk, sugar, salt and fish balls, bring to a boil and simmer for 2–3 minutes.

Meanwhile, blanch the bean sprouts in boiling water for 1 minute. Soak the vermicelli in warm water for 3 minutes, rinse and drain well. Divide the vermicelli into four bowls.

Add the shrimps to the soup and simmer for 2 minutes. Pour the soup into the bowls, garnish with shredded chicken, bean sprouts, cucumber, sliced chili and scallions. Serve immediately.

INGREDIENTS

8 shallots, sliced

3 cloves garlic, sliced

5 cm/2 in *galangal* or 1 inch fresh ginger, peeled and sliced

4 small red chilies, sliced

1 Tbsp chopped fresh lemon grass

5 Tbsp vegetable oil

2 tsp ground turmeric

1 tsp ground coriander

2 tsp dried shrimp paste (*belacan*) (optional)

100 g/4 oz bean curd (*tofu*), diced

2¼ cups/500 ml/18 fl oz light chicken stock

4¼ cups/1 litre/1¾ pt coconut milk (canned)

2 tsp sugar

2 tsp salt

2 fish balls, sliced

200 g/7 oz rice vermicelli

12 tiger or large shrimps, peeled and deveined

For the Garnish

cooked chicken from the light chicken broth, shredded

100 g/4 oz bean sprouts

5 cm/2 in cucumber, shredded

1 large red chili, sliced

2 scallions, chopped

2 cups/450 g1 lb *ramen* noodles, *or* 400 g/14 oz fresh *or* 11 oz dried thin egg noodles

6¼ cups/1.25 l/2¼ pt chicken broth

For the Spicy Sesame Sauce

1 Tbsp vegetable oil

2.5 cm/1 in fresh ginger, peeled and minced

3 cloves garlic, minced

220 g/8 oz pork, ground

8 shiitake mushrooms, minced

4 scallions, minced

6 Tbsp sesame sauce

5 Tbsp light soy sauce

1 Tbsp chili oil

EGG NOODLE SOUP WITH SPICY SESAME SAUCE

This is a famous Sichuan dish although it has gained popularity in other Asian countries. There are several versions to this recipe, but all include the rich aromatic sesame sauce which gives full flavor to the soup. You can adjust the amount of chili oil to your liking.

First, to make the spicy sesame sauce, heat the oil in a skillet. Fry the ginger and garlic for 30 seconds, add the pork, mushrooms and scallions, and stir-fry for 3–4 minutes.

Add the sesame sauce, soy sauce, chili oil and stir for 1–2 minutes. Set aside.

Boil plenty of water in a pan, add the noodles and cook for about 3 minutes or according to the instructions on the packet. Drain and divide into four bowls.

Heat the chicken broth. Pour the spicy sesame sauce over the noodles. Gently pour the broth into the bowls. Serve at once.

INGREDIENTS

1¾ cups/400 g/14 oz bean sprouts

2 cups/450 g/1 lb *ramen* noodles, *or*
400 g/14 oz fresh *or* 300 g/11 oz dried thin
egg noodles

6¼ cups/1.5 l/2½ pt *miso* sauce

½ sheet *nori* seaweed, cut into four

cress

For the Garnish

4 Tbsp sweetcorn

1 Tbsp spring onions

MISO RAMEN WITH BEAN SPROUTS

In this recipe, medium egg noodles are used but thin egg noodles can be used in their place if wished. When you blanch the bean sprouts take care not to overcook them. They should still be crispy when eaten.

Boil the water in a pan and blanch the bean sprouts for 30 seconds. Drain.

Boil plenty of water in a pan and add the noodles. Cook for 3 minutes and drain. Place the noodles in individual bowls.

Heat the *miso* sauce. Put a quarter of the bean sprouts, a square of *nori* and some cress on to each serving of noodles and pour the *miso* sauce over. Garnish with sweetcorn and spring onions and serve immediately.

Ingredients

1¾ cups/400 g/14 oz dried *soba*

1.5 l/2½ pt) *dashi* sauce

For the Topping

300 g/11 oz yam (*yama-imo*)

4 quails eggs

1 sheet of *nori* seaweed, shredded

3 spring onions, chopped

2 tsp *wasabi* mustard (optional)

Soba with Grated Yam

The yama-imo *or mountain potato is a Japanese member of the yam family.* Yama-imo *can be eaten as here, shreddedinto a thick, spongy topping. Japanese* yama-imo, *which tends not to discolor so quickly when peeled, is recommended for this dish.*

Heat the *dashi* sauce.

Bring plenty of water to a boil in a large pan and add the *soba*. Cook for 5–6 minutes. Drain and rinse well under cold water. Drain again. Divide into serving bowls.

Shred the yam peeling it as you go to stop it from slipping out of your fingers.

Put the shredded yam over the *soba*, then break the eggs into the center of the shredded yam. Sprinkle with *nori* and spring scallion. Put a ½ teaspoon of *wasabi* at the edge of each bowl.

Gently pour the *dashi* over and serve immediately.

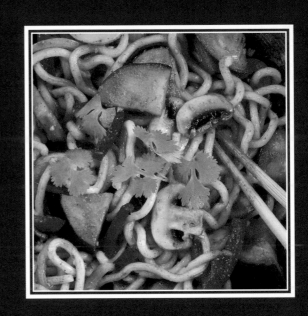

Chapter Two

Stir-Fried Noodles

Quick tasty dishes which
are easy to prepare and
ideal as lunchtime or
supper snacks.

Malaysian Fried Rice Noodles

If you are ever lucky enough to visit Malaysia, you will find this dish being sold in restaurants and from roadside stalls wherever you go. The fish balls in this recipe may not be available at supermarkets but you should be able to pick them up at oriental food stores.

Rinse the fresh flat rice noodles with warm water or soak the dried rice stick noodles in warm water for 2–5 minutes. Rinse and drain.

Heat 3 tablespoons of the oil in a wok or frying pan until very hot. Stir-fry the garlic and ginger for 30 seconds. Add the pork and fry for about 3 minutes. Add the chili and shrimps, then stir for about 1 minute. Add the sliced fish balls, bean sprouts and spinach and stir again for about 1 minute.

Make a well in the center, then add the egg. Scramble quickly. Add the remaining oil, and the rice noodles, sugar and soy sauce, then stir well. Taste and add the salt and black pepper. Put onto four plates and serve immediately.

4 cups/900 g/2 lb fresh flat rice noodles or 275 g/10 oz dried rice stick noodles

5 Tbsp vegetable oil

2 cloves garlic, finely chopped

1 cm/½ in ginger, peeled and finely chopped

175 g/6 oz boneless belly of pork or chicken breasts, skinned and thinly sliced

2 small red chilies, chopped

16 tiger or large shrimps with tails, peeled and deveined

8 fish balls, sliced or seafood sticks

1 cup/220 g/8 oz bean sprouts

½ cup/100 g/4 oz fresh spinach

2 eggs, beaten

1 tsp superfine sugar

3 Tbsp light soy sauce

3 Tbsp dark soy sauce

salt and black pepper

Spicy Rice Stick Noodles with Chicken

Authentic Thai spicy noodles are very hot indeed. The amount of green chili used in this recipe has been reduced to cool them down and save your taste buds! However, if you feel like increasing the spices, you can add more green chili if you dare.

If you use fresh noodles, just rinse with warm water. Soak dried rice noodles in warm water for 2–5 minutes or according to the instructions on the packet. Rinse and drain.

Heat 3 tablespoons of the oil in a wok or frying pan until very hot. Stir-fry the garlic and green chili for 30 seconds, then add the chicken and fry for about 3 minutes.

Add the string or snap beans, mustard greens or spinach and baby sweetcorn, stirring for 1–2 minutes. Add the remaining oil and the rice noodles and stir. Then add fish sauce, soy sauce and sugar and stir well.

Garnish with tomatoes and serve at once.

Ingredients

4 cups/900 g/2 lb fresh flat rice noodles *or* 280 g/10 oz dried rice stick noodles

5 Tbsp vegetable oil

2 cloves garlic, finely chopped

4–6 small green chilies, chopped

220 g/8 oz boneless chicken breasts, sliced into bite-sized pieces

½ cup/100 g/4 oz frozen string or snap beans, halved

½ cup/100 g/4 oz mustard greens *or* fresh spinach

16 tinned baby sweetcorn, each cut diagonally into 3 pieces

4 Tbsp fish sauce (*nam pla*)

2 Tbsp dark soy sauce

2 Tbsp light soy sauce

1 Tbsp palm or brown sugar

2 small tomatoes, halved

Stir-fried Noodles and Bean sprouts

Heat the oil in a wok over high heat. Add the onions and garlic and sauté for 2 minutes or so until the edges begin to brown.

Add the bean sprouts and stir-fry for 30 seconds. Add the noodles and stir-fry for 1 minute. Stir in the chicken broth and Nuoc Mam sauce and toss to combine. Add the scallions and remove from heat. Serve on a serving dish with cilantro and black pepper sprinkled all over.

INGREDIENTS

1 Tbsp vegetable oil

2 small onions, thinly sliced

4 cloves garlic, chopped

½ cup/100 g/4 oz bean sprouts

¾ cup/175 g/6 oz (dried weight) bean thread noodles, soaked in warm water for 30 minutes, drained and cut into 7.5 cm/3 in lengths

½ cup/110 ml/4 floz chicken broth

1 Tbsp Nuoc Mam sauce or light soy sauce

2 scallions, thinly sliced

1 Tbsp cilantro, chopped

freshly ground black pepper

INGREDIENTS

1¼ cups/300 g/11 oz dried egg noodles *or*
450 g/1 lb Japanese steamed noodles
1 Tbsp sesame oil
2 Tbsp sunflower oil
220 g/8 oz boneless belly of pork or chicken
breasts, thinly sliced
1 medium-sized onion, sliced
100 g/4 oz carrots, cut in half lengthwise and
thinly sliced
5 cabbage leaves, roughly cut
salt and black pepper
7 Tbsp *yakisoba* or Japanese brown sauce
nori flakes (*ao-nori*) (optional)
red pickled ginger (*beni-shouga*) (optional)

STIR-FRIED EGG NOODLES WITH YAKISOBA SAUCE

Maybe the most popular noodle dish eaten in Japan and found in noodle shops, at home, and made and served in the street at festivals or cooked over a camp fire for lunch during a trip out into the countryside. If yakisoba sauce is unavailable make your own.

If using dried noodles, boil plenty of water in a pan, add the noodles and cook for 3 minutes. Rinse with water and drain. Toss in the sesame oil. If you use Japanese steamed noodles, just rinse with very hot water.

Heat the sunflower oil in a wok or frying pan, then fry the pork for 3–4 minutes. Add the onion, carrots and cabbage and stir-fry for 3–4 minutes. Sprinkle with the salt and pepper, add the noodles and *yakisoba* or brown sauce and stir well.

Put the noodles onto four plates and sprinkle with the *nori* flakes and pickled ginger. Serve at once.

FRIED CELLOPHANE NOODLES WITH BEAN CURD

Bean curd is a favorite constituent of Thai cooking. This dish features fried bean curd. Like all types of bean curd, it is best to use what you buy in one go as it quickly deteriorates even if refrigerated.

Soak the cellophane noodles in boiling water for 5 minutes. Rinse under cold water and drain. Heat half the oil in a wok or frying pan and fry the bean curd until golden brown. Drain on absorbent paper.

Add the remaining oil to the wok, then fry the garlic and shallots for about 30 seconds. Add the bean sprouts, string or snap beans and scallions and stir well.

Add the cellophane noodles, bean curd, crushed peanuts, dried shrimps and green chili and stir. Season with the sugar, fish sauce and lemon juice, stirring again.

Divide the noodles onto four plates. Sprinkle with the crispy onions, cilantroleaves, red chili and garnish with a slice of lime. Serve at once.

INGREDIENTS

1 cup/220 g/8 oz cellophane noodles

4 Tbsp vegetable oil

275 g/10 oz bean curd (*tofu*), diced

3 cloves garlic, finely chopped

4 shallots, finely chopped

1 cup/200 g/7 oz bean sprouts

4 oz frozen string or snap beans, halved

2 scallions, chopped

2 Tbsp roasted peanuts, minced

2 Tbsp dried shrimps, chopped

3–5 small green chilies, chopped

2½ Tbsp palm or brown sugar

6 Tbsp fish sauce (*nam pla*)

½ cup/110 ml/4 floz freshly squeezed lemon juice

For the Garnish

2 tbsp crispy onion

cilantro

1 medium red chili, sliced

4 slices lime

INGREDIENTS

1¾ cups/400 g/14 oz dried or 560 g/1¼ lb parboiled fresh *udon*

3 Tbsp sunflower oil

¾ cup/175 g/6 oz squid, cleaned and sliced

¾ cup/175 g/6 oz peeled shrimps

4 scallions, chopped roughly

1 cup/220 g/8 oz bean sprouts

275 g/10 oz *shimeji* mushrooms, roots cut off and separated, or 15 *shiitake* mushrooms, sliced

4 tsp dried *wakame* seaweed, soaked in hot water

4 Tbsp bonito flakes (*katsuobushi*)

4 Tbsp Japanese soy sauce

salt and black pepper

STIR-FRIED UDON WITH SEAFOOD

Stir-frying coaxes maximum flavor out of the seafood ingredients and gives the udon *noodles a smooth, slippery texture in this filling dish.*

Boil plenty of water in a large pan and add the *udon*. Cook for 7–15 minutes for dried, or 3 minutes for parboiled fresh *udon*. Rinse under cold water and drain.

Heat the oil in a wok or frying pan until very hot. Stir-fry the squid and shrimps for 2 minutes. Add the scallions, bean sprouts, mushrooms and *wakame* and stir-fry for about 2 minutes.

Add the *udon*, bonito flakes and soy sauce and stir. Season with salt and pepper. Stir for another minute and serve at once.

Stir-fried Rice Vermicelli with Barbecued Pork and Shrimps

Another Chinese noodle dish using cha siu to provide extra flavor. If you do not have time to make cha siu, you can use sliced lean pork instead.

Soak the vermicelli in warm water for 3 minutes or according to the instructions on the packet. Rinse under cold water and drain.

Heat 3 tablespoons of the oil in a wok or large frying pan until very hot. Stir-fry the ginger and garlic for 30 seconds. Add the pork, shrimps, bean sprouts, water chestnuts, scallions and spinach and stir-fry for 2–3 minutes.

Add the remaining tablespoon of oil and the vermicelli, stir quickly, then add the rice wine, soy sauce and chicken broth. Keep stirring until the sauce is absorbed. Sprinkle with black pepper and salt to taste. Serve immediately.

INGREDIENTS

1 cup/220 g/8 oz rice vermicelli

4 Tbsp vegetable oil

2.5 cm/1 in fresh ginger, peeled and minced

2 cloves garlic, finely chopped

220 g/8 oz Chinese barbecued pork (*cha siu*), diced

100 g/4 oz peeled shrimps

1 cup/200 g/7 oz bean sprouts

8 water chestnuts, sliced

6 scallions chopped

100 g/4 oz spinach, chopped

2 Tbsp Chinese rice wine or dry sherry

4 Tbsp light soy sauce

1½ Tbsp dark soy sauce

6 Tbsp chicken broth

black pepper and salt

INGREDIENTS

1¼ cups/275 g/10 oz dried medium egg noodles

4 Tbsp + 2 tsp vegetable oil

1¼ cups/275 g/10 oz bean curd (*tofu*), diced

2 eggs, beaten

2.5 cm/1 in fresh ginger, peeled and finely chopped

4 shallots, minced

1 tsp ground coriander

1 red chili, chopped

220 g/8 oz boneless chicken breasts, diced

100 g/4 oz carrots, sliced

3 sticks celery, sliced

4 scallions, chopped into 2.5 cm/1 in lengths

3 Tbsp light soy sauce

salt and pepper

4 tomato wedges

sliced cucumber

INDONESIAN FRIED EGG NOODLES WITH CHICKEN AND BEAN CURD

Indonesian cooking has become increasingly popular over the last few years and mie goreng, *one of the most commonly eaten dishes in Indonesia, has been at the forefront of this trend.*

Cook the egg noodles in a pan of boiling water for 4 minutes. Rinse and drain well. Heat 1 tablespoon of the oil in a wok or frying pan and fry the bean curd until lightly browned. Set aside and clean the wok.

To make the egg sheets, heat 1 teaspoon of the oil in an omelet pan. Add half the beaten egg and fry both sides, like a thin pancake. Repeat to make a second egg sheet. When the egg sheets are cooled, slice them thinly.

Heat another 2 tablespoons of the oil in the wok, stir-fry the ginger, shallots, ground coriander and red chili for 30 seconds. Add the chicken and stir for 2–3 minutes. Add the carrots, celery, bean curd and scallions, stirring each time you add the ingredients.

Add the final tablespoon of oil, the noodles and soy sauce to the wok. Season with salt and pepper if required, and stir well. Divide the noodles onto four plates, sprinkle the sliced egg sheets on top and garnish with tomato wedges and cucumber slices. Serve at once.

INGREDIENTS

1¼ cups/275 g/10 oz dried rice stick noodles

4 Tbsp vegetable oil

1¼ cups/350 g/12 oz bean curd (*tofu*), diced

2.5 cm/1 in fresh ginger, peeled and finely chopped

2 cloves garlic, finely chopped

½ green pepper, diced

½ red pepper, diced

½ yellow pepper, diced

5 scallions, chopped

6 Tbsp black bean sauce

3 Tbsp light soy sauce

2 Tbsp Chinese rice wine or dry sherry

2 tsp superfine sugar

FRIED RICE STICK NOODLES WITH BEAN CURD AND BLACK BEAN SAUCE

Tofu *is prepared by cutting it into small cubes. Be careful when you do this as it is delicate stuff and prone to disintegrate if handled too roughly. Nutritious and healthy as it undoubtedly is,* tofu *will never win any awards for flavor, which is why its combination with the spicy, aromatic black bean sauce makes such a good pairing.*

Soak the rice stick noodles in warm water for **2–5** minutes, depending on the instructions on the packet. Rinse and drain.

Heat 3 tablespoons of the oil in a wok or frying pan. Fry the bean curd until golden brown. Add the ginger and garlic and stir. Add the peppers and scallions, and stir-fry for 1–2 minutes.

Add the remaining oil, noodles, black bean sauce, soy sauce, rice wine and sugar, then stir until the noodles are well coated with the sauce. Divide the noodles onto four plates and serve at once.

STIR-FRIED UDON WITH MISO SAUCE

This is another nouveau *stir-fried* udon *dish. The udon are coated in a salty sauce, making a very appetising fast food.*

Boil plenty of water in a large pan and cook dried *udon* for 7–15 minutes or parboiled fresh udon for 3 minutes. Rinse under cold water and drain.

Blanch the cabbage leaves and string or snapbeans for 2 minutes. Rinse under cold water. Cut the cabbage leaves into bite-sized pieces and halve the string or snap beans.

Heat the oil in a wok or frying pan until very hot. Add the beef and fry for 2–3 minutes. Add the cabbage, string or snap beans and shiitake mushrooms and sprinkle on salt and chilli powder. Stir-fry for another 2–3 minutes.

Mix the *miso*, soy sauce and *mirin* together in a bowl. Add the *udon* and *miso* mixture to the pan and stir-fry for about a minute. Put the *udon* onto four plates. Sprinkle the chopped scallion over and serve at once.

INGREDIENTS

1¾ cups/400 g/14 oz dried or 560 g/1¼ lb parboiled fresh *udon*

200 g/7 oz green cabbage

150 g/5 oz fresh green beans

3 Tbsp sunflower oil

220 g/8 oz rump steak, sliced on a slant into bite-sized pieces

1 small red bell pepper, chopped into bite-sized pieces

10 *shiitake* mushrooms, quartered

a pinch of salt and chili powder

2 Tbsp red *miso* paste

2 Tbsp Japanese soy sauce

2 Tbsp *mirin*

1 scallion, chopped

FRIED FLAT RICE NOODLES WITH BEEF AND BLACK BEAN SAUCE

Black bean sauce is just one of a number of end products that result from the fermentation of soya beans. Prepared with salt and spices, the black bean forms the basis of a very distinctive sauce to complement most meats. Here it is used with beef, but it makes an equally good companion to pork.

Rinse fresh flat rice noodles with hot water, or soak dried noodles in warm water for 2–5 minutes. Rinse and drain.

Marinate the beef with 1 tablespoon of the rice wine, 1 tablespoon of the soy sauce and the cornstarch for 30 minutes.

Heat 3 tablespoons of the oil in a wok or frying pan. Fry the beef for 2–3 minutes and set aside. Clean the wok.

Heat 2 tablespoons of the oil in a wok and stir-fry the ginger and garlic for 30 seconds. Add the scallion, onion and green bell pepper and stir until the onion becomes transparent.

Add the beef and noodles to the wok. Add the remaining oil, soy sauce and rice wine, the black bean sauce and the sugar. Stir well, until all the ingredients are thoroughly mixed. Divide the noodles onto four plates and serve.

INGREDIENTS

4 cups/900 g/2 lb fresh flat rice noodles *or* 1¼ cups/275 g/10 oz dried rice stick noodles

450 g/1 lb rump steak, sliced at a slant into bite-sized pieces

1 egg white

3 Tbsp Chinese rice wine or dry sherry

4 Tbsp light soy sauce

2 tsp cornstarch

7 Tbsp vegetable oil

2.5 cm/1 in fresh ginger, peeled and minced

3 cloves garlic, minced

2 scallions, chopped

2 medium-sized onions, cut into bite-sized squares

1 large green bell pepper, cut into bite-sized squares

6 Tbsp black bean sauce

2 tsp superfine sugar

STIR-FRIED EGG NOODLES WITH VEGETABLES

Boil plenty of water in a pan and cook the noodles for 3–4 minutes. Rinse under cold water and drain.

Heat the vegetable oil in a wok or frying pan, then stir-fry the ginger and garlic for 30 seconds. Add the Chinese cabbage, bean sprouts, red and green bell peppers and straw mushrooms. Stir each ingredient as you add it. Fry together for about 2 minutes.

Add the sesame oil, noodles, scallions, soy sauce and sugar and stir well. Check the taste, adding salt and pepper if necessary. Put the noodles onto four plates and serve at once.

INGREDIENTS

2 cups/450 g/1 lb fresh or 10 oz dried medium egg noodles
2 Tbsp vegetable oil
2.5 cm/1 in fresh ginger, peeled and minced
2 cloves garlic, minced
1¼ cups/275 g/10 oz Chinese cabbage, chopped into bite-sized squares
1 cup/200 g/7 oz bean sprouts
1 small red bell pepper, cut into bite-sized squares
1 small green bell pepper, cut into bite-sized squares
16 straw mushrooms (canned), halved
1 Tbsp sesame oil
2 scallions, chopped
4 Tbsp light soy sauce
1 Tbsp dark soy sauce
1 Tbsp superfine sugar
salt and black pepper

SINGAPORE SPICY NOODLES

The return home of itinerant Chinese over the years has resulted in a gradual increase in the popularity of curried dishes in China, especially in the south-western provinces. Although the origins of this dish lie in India, Singapore has been the cultural melting pot where most Chinese migrants have come into contact with Indian cuisine.

Soak the rice vermicelli in warm water for 3 minutes or according to the instructions on the packet. Rinse with cold water and drain.

Heat 3 tablespoons of the oil in a wok or frying pan until very hot. Add the garlic, ginger and red chili and stir-fry for 30 seconds.

Add the shrimps and squid and stir for another minute. Then add the bean sprouts, spinach and pork and stir-fry for 1–2 minutes.

Make a well in the center, add the beaten egg and scramble lightly. Quickly add the remaining tablespoon of oil and the rice vermicelli and mix all the ingredients well.

Add the scallion, salt, chili powder, black pepper. curry powder, soy sauce, superfine sugar and chicken broth. Stir until the sauce is all absorbed. Put the noodles onto four plates and serve at once.

1 cup/220 g/8 oz rice vermicelli

4 Tbsp vegetable oil

2 cloves garlic, minced

1 cm/¼ in fresh ginger, peeled and minced

1 red chili, chopped

100 g/4 oz peeled shrimps

6 small squid, cleaned and sliced

1 cup/220 g/8 oz bean sprouts

4 oz spinach

1 cup/220 g/8 oz Chinese barbecued pork (*cha siu*), thinly sliced

2 eggs, beaten

3 scallions, roughly chopped

⅔ tsp salt

a pinch of chili powder

black pepper

2–3 tsp hot curry powder

1 Tbsp light soy sauce

2 tsp superfine sugar

½ cup/150 ml/¼ pt chicken broth

INGREDIENTS

1¾ cups/450 g/1 lb fresh *or* 10 oz dried medium egg noodles

3 Tbsp vegetable oil

2.5 cm/1 in fresh ginger, peeled and minced

3 cloves garlic, minced

½ cup/110 g/4 oz peeled shrimps

12 tiger or large shrimps, peeled and deveined

1 small red bell pepper, sliced

4 scallions, chopped into 2.5 cm/1 in lengths

black pepper

1 Tbsp sesame oil

4 tsp light soy sauce

4 tsp dark soy sauce

2 Tbsp Chinese rice wine or dry sherry

3 Tbsp black bean sauce

STIR-FRIED EGG NOODLES WITH SHRIMPS AND BLACK BEAN SAUCE

These stir-fried noodles require cooking for only a short time. Tiger shrimps add both flavor and a certain luxury to this dish, so if you are feeling extravagant, use them in place of their smaller cousins.

Cook the noodles in a pan of boiling water for 4 minutes. Rinse and drain well.

Heat the vegetable oil in a wok or frying pan. stir-fry the ginger and garlic for 30 seconds. Add the shrimps, red bell pepper, scallions and a sprinkling of black pepper and stir for 1–2 minutes or until the shrimps are heated thoroughly.

Add the sesame oil and noodles and stir. Add the soy sauce, rice wine and black bean sauce, then stir again until the noodles are coated well with the sauce.

Put the noodles onto four plates and serve at once.

STIR-FRIED VERMICELLI WITH VEGETABLES

Heat the oil in a wok over high heat and fry the garlic until golden brown. Add the carrot and stir-fry for 1 minute.

Add all the remaining ingredients except the vermicelli, stirring gently. Cook for 2 minutes.

Add the vermicelli and toss to combine all the ingredients. Stir for 1 minute. Serve in a large serving dish.

1 Tbsp vegetable oil

1 clove garlic, minced

1 carrot, thinly sliced

¼ cup/50 ml/2 fl oz water

¼ cup/50 g/2 oz Chinese cabbage, shredded

½ celery stick, shredded

3 Tbsp chicken broth

1 Tbsp oyster sauce

1 Tbsp Nuoc Mam sauce *or* 1 Tbsp light soy sauce and ½ tsp anchovy essence

1 level tsp sugar

freshly ground black pepper

½ cup/100 g/4 oz rice vermicelli, soaked in warm water for 5 minutes and drained well

CHAPTER THREE

VEGETABLES AND RICE

A VARIETY OF DISHES SUITABLE
FOR BUFFETS, DINNER PARTY
SIDE DISHES OR A
QUICK LUNCH.

SUMMER AVOCADO

Peel the avocados. Cut them in half and remove the stones. Cut the flesh in slices and pour on the lemon juice to prevent discoloration.

Using a small sharp knife, cut a slice from the grapefruit exposing the flesh. Cut round in strips removing all the white pith.

When the grapefruit are peeled and showing no pith, cut into each section between the membranes of each slice. At the end you will have segments of grapefruit without skin. Squeeze the juice of the membranes by hand over the fruit.

Line individual dishes with washed, drained lettuce leaves and cucumber slices.

Pour some of the Vinaigrette Dressing over the grapefruit.

Mix the cooked shrimps with the rice and dressing.

Cut the yellow bell pepper in thin strips. Retaining some for garnishing, chop the remainder and mix with the rice and shrimps. Season well.

Arrange the shrimp and rice mixture in the dishes on the cucumber and lettuce.

Top with sliced avocado and grapefruit. Garnish with bell pepper rings.

2 ripe avocados

1 Tbsp lemon juice

2 grapefruit

1 small lettuce

¼ cucumber

½ cup/150 ml/¼ pt Vinaigrette Dressing

½ cup/100 g/4 oz cooked shrimps

¼ cup/50 g/2 oz yellow long-grain rice, cooked

1 yellow bell pepper, seeded

salt and freshly ground black bell pepper

Ingredients

2 cups/220 g/8 oz long-grain rice, cooked

½ cup/150 ml/1¼ pt Vinaigrette Dressing

8 scallions, washed

4 large slices of cooked ham

8 fresh or canned asparagus spears

a few lettuce leaves or watercress

½ cup/150 ml/¼ pt mayonnaise

Ham and Asparagus Salad

This is a quick and easy buffet dish or it can be served as a starter or easy lunch.

Mix the rice with the dressing in a bowl. Mince the scallions and mix with the rice.

Lay the ham flat on a board. Place 2 asparagus spears on the ham and roll up.

Lay dressed rice on a bed of lettuce or surround with watercress. Arrange the rolls of ham on top and serve with mayonnaise in a jug.

INGREDIENTS

2 cups/220 g/8 oz rice

1 tsp salt

1 tsp garam masala

1 tsp turmeric

1 bay leaf

25 g/1 oz butter

1 clove garlic, minced

1 onion, peeled and diced

½ cup/50 g/2 oz golden raisins

1 green bell pepper, seeded, blanched and diced

Garnish

6 Tbsp low-fat yogurt

2 scallions, washed

SPICED RICE SALAD

Cook the rice in boiling salted water with the garam masala, turmeric and bay leaf for about 15 minutes until tender.

Meanwhile melt the butter and gently sweat the garlic and onion without browning for 5 minutes.

Add the garlic and onion to the rice when it is cooked and allow it to cool.

Stir in the golden raisins and bell pepper.

Garnish with chopped scallions. Stir in yogurt before serving.

INGREDIENTS

225 g/8 oz small broccoli florets

100 g/4 oz fine asparagus spears

225 g/8 oz savoy cabbage, shredded

1.1 1/2 pts vegetable stock

50 g/2 oz garlic and herb butter

4 trimmed and shredded small leeks

400 g/14 oz arborio rice

salt and ground black pepper

4 Tbsp chopped fresh parsley

GREEN VEGETABLE RISOTTO

SERVES 4

This dish makes an excellent accompaniment to meat or fish dishes, and can also be served as a vegetarian main meal.

Bring a saucepan of water to the boil and cook the broccoli for 3 to 4 minutes until just tender; cook the asparagus and cabbage for 1 minute until just tender. Drain the vegetables and set aside. Reserve the cooking water and use to make up the stock.

Pour the stock into a saucepan and bring to the boil. Reduce the heat to a gentle simmer.

Meanwhile, melt the garlic and herb butter in a large saucepan and gently fry the leeks for 2 to 3 minutes until softened but not browned. Stir in the rice and cook, stirring, for 2 minutes until the rice is well coated in the leek mixture.

Add a ladleful of stock and cook gently over moderate heat, stirring, until absorbed. Season well. Continue adding the stock until the risotto becomes thick, but not sticky, and the rice is tender. This will take about 25 minutes.

Stir in the cooked vegetables and chopped parsley, and heat through for 2 to 3 minutes until hot. Serve immediately.

BLUE CHEESE RICE QUICHE

Make up the pastry by sifting the flour and salt into a bowl. Add the fat in small lumps and rub in with the finger tips until the mixture resembles fine breadcrumbs. Add the water, a few drops at a time, and mix to a firm dough. Rest in the refrigerator for 15 minutes.

Roll the pastry out in a neat circle to fit a 7-in flan ring. Lift the pastry on to the rolling pin and over the ring. Then ease it in to avoid stretching. Trim the top with the rolling pin. Line with waxed paper and some baking beans. Bake in the preheated oven for 15 minutes at the higher temperature. Remove the paper and baking beans and cook for a further 5 minutes. Allow to cool slightly.

Arrange the rice in the bottom of the flan. Mix the crumbled blue cheese with the rice. Beat the eggs in a cup. Add the cream and seasonings. Pour over the rice and cheese. Sprinkle with chopped parsley. Bake for 20 minutes at the lower temperature until set and golden. Oven temperatures 400°F/350°F

INGREDIENTS

Shortcrust Pastry

1 cup/110 g/4 oz all-purpose flour

a pinch of salt

25 g/1 oz butter or margarine

25 g/1 oz white fat

1½ Tbsp cold water

Filling

½ cup/50 g/2 oz cooked long-grain rice

½ cup/75 g/3 oz blue cheese, crumbled

2 eggs

2 Tbsp light cream

salt and freshly ground black bell pepper

a pinch of cayenne bell pepper

¼ tsp dry mustard

2 tsp chopped parsley

oven temperatures 400°F/350°F

Waldorf Rice Salad

Cook the rice until fluffy, forking from time to time to separate the grains. Allow to cool.

Add the minced onion to the rice and mix well.

Remove the strings from the celery stalks and mince. Add to the rice.

Add the chopped scallions and walnuts to the rice and mix well.

Chop part of both apples into small cubes, sprinkle with lemon juice and mix with the rice salad, mayonnaise and parsley.

Decorate with remaining apple slices and walnut halves.

INGREDIENTS

2 cups/220 g/8 oz long-grain rice

1 small onion, peeled and minced

6 stalks celery, washed

4 scallions, washed and chopped

½ cup/50 g/2 oz walnuts, chopped

1 red apple

1 green apple

½ cup/150 ml/¼ pt mayonnaise

1 Tbsp fresh parsley

juice of 1 lemon

INGREDIENTS

2 Tbsp groundnut oil

7 cups/800 g/1¾ lb cooked rice

3 Tbsp phrik nam plaa sauce

FRIED RICE WITH SPICY SAUCE

Nam phrik gives this dish flavor and nutritional value. A tasty lunchtime dish.

Heat the oil in a wok or pan, add the rice and mix well, stir-frying for 1 minute. Add the sauce, mix well and cook for 1 more minute. Remove from the heat.

Serve accompanied by preserved salted eggs, cucumber slices, fried eggs and raw vegetables.

BEAN SPROUT AND RICE SALAD

INGREDIENTS

¾ cup/175 g/6 oz can bean sprouts

1 Tbsp vegetable oil

1 Tbsp soy sauce

1 small piece of root ginger, minced

salt and freshly ground bell pepper

6 scallions

1 cup/110 g/4 oz cooked long-grain rice

4 Tbsp salad oil

2 Tbsp lemon juice

½ tsp sugar

4 slices of Chinese leaves

Drain the can of bean sprouts. Heat the vegetable oil in a small saucepan. Toss in the bean sprouts with the soy sauce and minced ginger. Stir well. Cover and cook for 3 minutes on a low heat.

Turn the bean sprouts into a bowl and allow to cool. Season well.

Chop the scallions into small pieces and add to the cooled bean sprouts. Retain a few pieces for garnish.

Stir in the rice.

Mix the salad oil with the lemon juice in a screw-top jar.

Arrange the Chinese leaves in the bottom of the salad bowl. Shake the oil and lemon juice dressing and pour over the bean sprouts and rice. Mix well and arrange in the salad bowl.

Garnish with a few rings of chopped scallions.

Stuffed Tomatoes

Ingredients

4 large tomatoes

½ cup/50 g/2 oz long-grain rice, cooked

salt and freshly ground bell pepper

2 Tbsp oil

1 large onion, peeled

1 green bell pepper, seeded and sliced

1 chili bell pepper, seeded and sliced

½ tsp curry powder (optional)

¼ cup/25 g/1 oz almonds, chopped

1 tsp cilantro or chopped parsley

2 oz/50 g/2 oz cooked minced beef, lamb or chicken

Remove the top of the tomatoes. Scoop out the centers into a bowl.

Add the cooked long-grain rice. Season well.

Heat the oil and fry the onion over a low heat for 3 minutes. Add the sliced bell pepper and chili. Sprinkle with the curry powder and continue cooking for 2 minutes. Add the chopped almonds.

Finally sprinkle in the chopped cilantro or parsley. Add the meat and mix well.

Fill each tomato with the rice mixture. Brush the tomatoes with oil. Then cook in the oven for about 15 minutes. Oven temperature 180°C/350°F

Spicy Okra

Remove the little end pieces of the okra. Heat 3 tablespoons of the oil in a frying pan and fry until golden for 2 minutes. Remove from the pan.

Blend 1 tablespoon oil, the onion, chili, cumin and coriander seeds with the garlic in a food processor or blender. Add a few drops of water if too thick.

Heat the oil again in the pan and fry the paste on a fairly high heat for about 2 minutes. Lower the heat. Add the okra, chopped tomatoes, salt, sugar and lemon juice. Add the water and simmer for 10–15 minutes.

Accompany with curry dishes and rice.

INGREDIENTS

450 g/1 lb okra

4 Tbsp oil

1 large onion, peeled and chopped

1 chili bell pepper, seeded and chopped

2 tsp cumin seeds

2 tsp coriander seeds

2 cloves garlic, peeled and minced

2 tomatoes, peeled and chopped or approx

¾ cup/175 g/6 oz can peeled tomatoes

¼ tsp salt

¼ tsp sugar

2 tbsp lemon juice

½ cup/150 ml/¼ pt water

CHILI BEAN RISOTTO

SERVES 4

Packed full of the flavors of Mexico, this tasty risotto makes a substantial main meal served on its own.

Pour the stock into a saucepan and bring to the boil. Reduce the heat to a gentle simmer.

Meanwhile, heat the oil in a large saucepan and gently fry the onion, garlic, chili and green peppers for 4 to 5 minutes until softened, but not browned. Stir in the rice and cook, stirring, for 2 minutes until the rice is coated in the vegetable mixture.

Add a ladleful of stock and cook gently, stirring, until absorbed. Continue adding the stock ladle-by-ladle until half the stock is used. Stir in the spices, seasoning and kidney beans.

Continue adding the stock until the risotto becomes thick, but not sticky. This will take about 25 minutes and shouldn't be hurried.

Stir in the sweetcorn and tomatoes. Mix well, adjust seasoning if necessary, and serve.

1,1 1/2 pts vegetable stock

2 Tbsp vegetable oil

1 large onion, finely chopped

1 garlic clove, crushed

1 green chili, seeded and finely chopped

2 green peppers, seeded and diced

400 g/14 oz arborio rice

1 tsp ground cumin

1 tsp ground coriander

1 tsp chilli powder

salt and ground black pepper

400 g/14 oz can kidney beans, drained and rinsed

350 g/12 oz can sweetcorn, drained and rinsed

4 medium tomatoes, peeled, seeded and chopped

INGREDIENTS

1.1 1/2 pts vegetable stock

75 g/3 oz butter

2 medium red onions, finely chopped

2 garlic cloves, crushed

450 g/1 lb butternut squash flesh, diced

400 g/14 oz arborio rice

salt and ground black pepper

150 ml/¼ pt dry white wine

400 g/14 oz can chopped tomatoes

2 Tbsp chopped fresh parsley

RISOTTO WITH SQUASH
SERVES 4

Squash combines with tomatoes in this buttery risotto. Serve this as an unusual accompaniment to a casserole, or as a delicious main meal.

Pour the stock into a saucepan and bring to a boil. Reduce the heat to a gentle simmer.

Meanwhile, melt the butter and gently fry the onion, garlic and squash for 7 to 8 minutes until just softening. Add the rice and cook, stirring, for 2 minutes until well mixed. Season well.

Add the wine and chopped tomatoes and cook gently, stirring, until absorbed. Add the stock, ladle-by-ladle, until the liquid is absorbed and the rice is thick, creamy and tender. Keep the heat moderate. This will take about 25 minutes.

Adjust seasoning if necessary. Serve sprinkled with chopped parsley.

Stuffed Zucchinis

Ingredients

4 large zucchinis

1 onion, peeled

1 red bell pepper, seeded

1 green bell pepper, seeded

4 Tbsp vegetable oil

1 clove garlic, minced

1 cup/100 g/4 oz cooked long-grain rice

100 g/4 oz cooked chicken (optional)

2 Tbsp cooked corn

¼ tsp cumin

½ tsp garam masala

salt and freshly ground bell pepper

½ cup/150 ml/¼ pt sour cream

1 Tbsp chopped parsley

Wash the zucchinis and cut a thin slice lengthwise across the top of each. Scoop out the flesh and chop into small pieces. Cut a small slice off the bottom if any of the zucchinis are tipping over when laid flat.

Prepare the vegetables by dicing the onion and bell peppers. Heat the oil in a skillet and cook the onion for 3 minutes. Then add the bell peppers and garlic. Cook for a further 3 minutes.

Add the rice and stir well. If you are using chicken, dice and add at this stage. Sprinkle in the corn and the seasonings over a low heat and mix for 1 minute.

Brush the zucchini shells with oil and fill with the rice mixture. Pour the sour cream over and bake in the oven for 20 minutes.

Sprinkle with chopped parsley. Oven temperature 180°C/350°F

INGREDIENTS

450 g/1 lb frozen leaf spinach *or* 900 g/2 lb
fresh spinach, washed
25 g/1 oz butter
1 Tbsp oil
1 medium onion, peeled
1 leek, washed and trimmed
juice of ½ lemon
salt and freshly ground bell pepper
2 cups/220 g/8 oz long-grain rice
2½ cups/570 ml/1 pt water or broth
¼ tsp nutmeg
1 Tbsp chopped fresh parsley

Topping

1 Tbsp natural yogurt (optional)

SAVORY SPINACH AND RICE

Cook the frozen spinach as directed on the packet or, if thawed, simmer for a few minutes in 4 tablespoons water. Drain well in a colander, squeezing out excess moisture with the back of a wooden spoon. If using fresh spinach remove thick stems, tear into manageable pieces and cook in 1.2 cm (½ in) boiling water for 4 minutes. Drain well.

Heat the butter and oil over a low heat in a large saucepan. Slice the onion and leek finely and cook in the fat for 4–5 minutes. Sprinkle with lemon juice and seasoning.

Add the long-grain rice and stir in with the vegetables. Add a boiling water or broth mixed with ½ teaspoon salt and pour over the rice and vegetables. Cover with a tight-fitting lid and simmer for 15 minutes. Remove the lid. Fluff the rice with a fork and add the spinach, nutmeg and chopped parsley. Mix with a fork, cover and reheat for 5 minutes.

Yogurt may be spooned over. This dish goes well with meats or fish or it can be served simply as a vegetarian dish.

PINEAPPLE RICE

INGREDIENTS

1 pineapple

4 Tbsp groundnut oil

5 cups/550 g/1¼ lb cooked rice

75 g/3 oz finely diced ham

½ Tbsp chopped garlic

½ cup/50 g/2 oz raisins

2 Tbsp chicken broth

2 tsp curry powder

1 tsp sugar

1 tsp salt

¼ tsp ground white bell pepper

A 'show-off' dish that is quite easy to make but always impressive to present. Although the pineapple also adds flavor to the rice, there is scarcely any point attempting it just with pineapple pieces – appearance is everything.

Cut one side off the pineapple lengthwise to expose the inside. Carefully remove the inside fruit and cut into small dice.

Reserve the outside of the pineapple.

Heat the oil in a pan or wok, add the ham and garlic, stir-fry, then add 75 g/3 oz of the diced pineapple and all the rest of the ingredients. Mix well. Spoon into the empty pineapple, cover with the pineapple lid and bake in a preheated 140°C/275°F oven for 30 minutes.

INGREDIENTS

1.1 1/2 pt vegetable stock

2 Tbsp olive oil

1 large onion, finely chopped

1 garlic clove, crushed

400 g/14 oz arborio rice

1 tsp dried mixed herbs

⅔ cup/150 ml/¼ pt red wine

400 g/14 oz can chopped tomatoes

salt and ground black pepper

150 g/5 oz stoned black olives

2 Tbsp capers

Romano cheese shavings, to garnish

OLIVE, CAPER AND TOMATO RISOTTO

SERVES 4

The traditional combination of ingredients in this dish gives a thoroughly Italian flavour to this risotto.

Pour the stock into a saucepan and bring to the boil. Reduce the heat to a gentle simmer.

Meanwhile, heat the oil in a large saucepan and gently fry the onion and garlic for 2 to 3 minutes until softened but not browned. Add the rice and herbs and cook, stirring, for 2 minutes until well coated in the onion mixture.

Add the wine and chopped tomatoes and cook gently, stirring, until absorbed. Ladle in the stock gradually and cook until all the liquid is absorbed and the rice is thick, creamy and tender.

Season well and stir in the olives and capers. Serve topped with shavings of Romano cheese and sprinkled with black pepper.

INGREDIENTS

2 cups/220 g/8 oz long-grain rice

2½ cups/570 ml/1 pt water

½ tsp salt

4 Tbsp oil

25 g/1 oz butter

2 onions, peeled and minced

2 cloves garlic, crushed

salt and freshly ground black bell pepper

2 red bell peppers, seeded and blanched

4 zucchinis, washed and thinly sliced

½ tsp basil

4 Tbsp white wine

8 tomatoes, skinned and chopped

Garnish

1 Tbsp chopped capers

2 hard-boiled eggs

8 green olives, pitted

2 Tbsp chopped fresh parsley

RICE À LA PROVENÇALE

This is a useful recipe to serve with many main dishes as there is no need to cook separate vegetables.

Cook the long-grain rice in 2½ cups/570 ml/1 pt water with ½ teaspoon salt, by bringing the water to a boil, adding the rice and stirring to separate the grains. Cover and simmer gently until the water has all been absorbed, which will take about 15 minutes.

Heat the oil and butter and cook the onions over a low heat for about 4 minutes.

Add the garlic. Dice the blanched bell peppers and add with the sliced zucchinis, the basil and white wine. Stir gently until cooked for about 5 minutes. Lastly stir in the tomatoes. Gently fold in the cooked rice and season well.

Add the chopped capers and turn into a heated serving dish.

Decorate with hard-cooked eggs, green olives and chopped herbs.

Chapter Four

Cold Noodle Dishes

A RANGE OF RECIPES USING
CHILLED NOODLES WITH
EITHER HOT OR COLD SAUCES
AND TOPPINGS.

CHILLED SOBA WITH NAMEKO MUSHROOMS

A light, refreshing lunch or part of a dinner that is quickly prepared and easily digested.

Boil plenty of water in a large pan and add the *soba*. Cook for 5–6 minutes or according to the instruction on the packet. Rinse under the tap and drain well. Put the *soba* into four bowls.

Mix the mushrooms and *mooli* or *daikon* together in a bowl. Pile them on to the *soba* and sprinkle with the *nori*. Gently pour the chilled dipping sauceover just before serving.

INGREDIENTS

1¾ cups/400 g/14 oz dried *soba*
approx 400 g/14 oz can *nameko* mushrooms
300 g/11 oz *mooli* or *daikon*, peeled and grated
½ sheet *nori* seaweed, shredded
2¼ cups/500 ml/18 floz dipping sauce, chilled

INGREDIENTS

¾ cup/200 g/7 oz cellophane noodles

16 tiger shrimps, peeled and deveined

1 tsp fish sauce (*nam pla*)

2 tsp freshly squeezed lemon juice

1 tsp palm or brown sugar

1 Tbsp sunflower oil

1 small red bell pepper, minced

2 sticks celery, thinly sliced

100 g/4 oz carrots, cut into matchsticks

2 scallions, chopped

4–5 lettuce leaves

cilantro

Dressing

2 shallots, minced

1 dry red chilli, crushed

3 small green chilli, chopped

4 Tbsp fish sauce (*nam pla*)

½ cup/110 ml/4 floz freshly squeezed lemon

juice (about

2 lemons)

4½ Tbsp palm or brown sugar

1 Tbsp sunflower oil

CELLOPHANE NOODLE SALAD WITH SHRIMPS

Yam woonsen is a hot Thai salad. Nam pla*, an essential ingredient used in Thai cuisine, enhances the flavor of the dish. It is a good idea to prepare this salad at least 30 minutes before you serve it to allow the full sweet, hot flavor to mature.*

Soak the cellophane noodles in warm water for 5 minutes or according to the instructions on the packet. Rinse under cold running water and drain.

Marinate the shrimps in 1 teaspoon of fish sauce, 2 teaspoons of lemon and 1 teaspoon of sugar for 15 minutes.

Mix together the dressing ingredients.

Heat 1 tablespoon of oil in a frying pan and stir-fry the shrimps thoroughly.

Put the red bell pepper, celery, carrot, scallions and noodles in a bowl and mix together. Place 1 lettuce leaf on each plate and pile the noodle mixture on it. Put the shrimps on the noodles and sprinkle over the cilantro.

Serve the dressing seperately.

Chilled Egg Noodles with Chicken and Pepperoni

Pepperoni is not an authentic topping, but it really goes well with chilled noodles and gives an extra punch to this dish.

Boil plenty of water in a pan and add the noodles. Cook for 3 minutes and rinse under the tap. Drain, then toss in the sesame oil. Put into four shallow dishes.

To prepare the sauce, heat the broth, soy sauce and sugar in a pan and simmer for 3 minutes. Turn off the heat and add the vinegar, 4 teaspoons sesame oil and ginger juice. Mix well before chiling in the refrigerator.

Boil the chicken in a pan for about 15–20 minutes. Let it cool and pull into shreds with your fingers or a knife. Set aside. Keep the water in the pan as broth for another use.

Mix the beaten egg and sugar together in a bowl. Heat 1 teaspoon of oil in an omelet pan and pour a third of the egg mixture into it. When the egg is half set, turn it over. Repeat this to make two more thin omelets, using fresh oil each time. When the omelets are cooled, cut them in half and shred.

Arrange the chicken, egg, cucumber and pepperoni on the noodles. Put the red pickled ginger (if using) on top and sprinkle with the sesame seeds. Pour the chilled sauce over prior to eating.

INGREDIENTS

450 g/1 lb fresh *or* 300 g/11 oz dried thin egg noodles
1 Tbsp sesame oil

Sauce

1 cup/250 ml/9 floz chicken broth
½ cup/110 ml/4 floz light soy sauce
4 Tbsp superfine sugar
½ cup/110 ml/4 floz vinegar
4 tsp sesame oil
2 Tbsp squeezed ginger juice

Topping

2 boneless chicken breasts
2 eggs, beaten
2 tsp superfine sugar
1 Tbsp vegetable oil
13 cm/5 in cucumber, thinly sliced diagonally and cut into long matchsticks
8 slices pepperoni, cut into long matchsticks
4 tsp red pickled ginger (*beni-shouga*) (optional)
4 tsp toasted sesame seeds

Toasted Sesame Seeds

This is very easy to do. Just roast the sesame seeds in a frying pan without any oil. When the sesame seeds puff up and you can smell their aromatic flavor, they are ready. It is a good idea to roast a large amount of seeds and keep them in a jar for future use.

CHILLED UDON WITH FERMENTED SOYA BEANS

Fermented soya beans, or natto, are not to everyone's taste. Even in Japan, where it originated, natto is very much a "love it or hate it" food despite it being a nutritious source of protein. Give it a try. You never know – you might like it! Natto is available from Japanese food stores.

Remove the tiny hairs on the okra, the easiest way to do this is to first sprinkle the salt over the okra and roll it over on a chopping board. Blanch in the boiling water for 1 minute, drain and chop.

Mix the okra, natto, bonito flakes, scallions, mustard and soy sauce together in a bowl.

Bring plenty of water to the boil in a large pan and add the udon. Cook according to the instructions on the packet. Rinse and drain. Divide the udon into four bowls.

Pile the natto mixture on top of the udon. Gently pour the dipping sauce over and sprinkle with nori, then serve immediately.

INGREDIENTS

1¾ cups/400 g/14 oz dried or 1¼ lb parboiled fresh udon
2¼ cups/500 ml/18 floz dipping sauce, chilled

Topping

6 okra
salt
1 cup/200 g/7 oz Japanese fermented soya beans (natto)
5 g/¼ oz bonito flakes (katsuo bushi)
1 scallion, chopped
1 tsp hot prepared mustard
4 tsp Japanese soy sauce
½ sheet nori, shredded

CHILLED SOBA WITH SHREDDED DAIKON

Japanese daikon *is the ideal ingredient for this dish but is quite hard to come by unless there happens to be a Japanese food store nearby. I find that* mooli *makes an acceptable stand-in.*

Bring plenty of water to a boil in a large saucepan. Add the *soba* and cook for 5–6 minutes. Rinse and cool in cold water. Drain.

Mix the *soba, daikon* and cress well in a bowl. Divide into individual serving bowls and sprinkle with the *nori.* Serve with the chilled dipping sauce and garnishes on a separate small dish.

INGREDIENTS

1¾ cups/400 g/14 oz dried *soba*

300 g/11 oz *daikon* or *mooli*, peeled and shredded

cress, rinsed

1 sheet *nori* seaweed, shredded

3 cups/725 ml/1¼ pt dipping sauce

Garnishes

2 scallions, chopped

2.5 cm/1 in fresh ginger, shredded

2 *myoga* (optional), shredded

INGREDIENTS

2¼ cups/500 ml/18 fl oz *dashi* sauce

4 Tbsp vinegar

1¾ cups/400 g/14 oz dried or 560 g/1¼ lb parboiled fresh *udon*

Topping

1 tbsp sunflower oil

2 cloves garlic, minced

1 cm/½ in fresh ginger, peeled and minced

8 scallions, chopped

200 g/7 oz eggplant, cut into matchsticks sized pieces and soaked in salted water

200 g/7 oz small green bell pepper, cut into matchsticks

a pinch of salt

4 Tbsp *miso* paste

1 Tbsp Japanese soy sauce

2 tsp superfine sugar

3 Tbsp Japanese rice wine (*sake*)

CHILLED UDON WITH EGGPLANT AND MISO SAUCE

Miso *sauce is a versatile performer that can be paired with almost any vegetable you care to mention. Here it is combined with eggplant which should be treated with salt to remove any trace of bitterness.*

Mix the *dashi* sauce and vinegar and chill in the refrigerator. Heat the oil in a frying pan. Add the garlic, ginger and scallion and fry for one minute.

Add the eggplant, green bell pepper and salt and stir-fry for 4–5 minutes or until the eggplant is softened. Add the *miso* paste, soy sauce, sugar and *sake* and stir well. Set aside.

Boil plenty of water in a pan and add the *udon*. Cook for 4–5 minutes for fresh or 8–15 minutes for dried *udon* or according to the instruction on the packet. Rinse with cold water. Drain and divide into four bowls.

Place the eggplant mixture on the *udon* and pour the sauce over. Serve immediately.

CHILLED EGG NOODLES WITH CHICKEN AND PEANUT SAUCE

A well-loved Chinese noodle dish. It can be prepared with any type of peanut butter, depending on your preference for smooth or crunchy.

Put the chicken in a large pan of water. Bring to a boil and simmer for 20 minutes, skimming off the scum from time to time. The poaching water can be put towards making broth. When the chicken is cooled, shred with your fingers or with a knife.

Mix the peanut butter, sugar, vinegar, chicken broth, soy sauce, sesame oil and chili oil together in a bowl.

Bring a large pan of water to a boil and add the noodles. Cook for 3 minutes, rinse and drain. Toss in the sesame oil. Put the noodles on the individual plates.

Place a quarter of the shredded chicken and cucumber on each serving of noodles. Pour the sesame sauce over and serve immediately.

INGREDIENTS

450 g/1 lb boneless chicken breasts

2 cups/450 g/1 lb fresh thin egg noodles

2 tsp sesame oil

25 cm/10 in cucumber, thinly sliced diagonally, then cut into long matchsticks

Peanut Sauce

8 Tbsp peanut butter

6 Tbsp superfine sugar

4 Tbsp vinegar

5 Tbsp chicken broth

3 Tbsp light soy sauce

1 Tbsp dark soy sauce

4 tsp sesame oil

3–4 tsp chili oil

CHAPTER FIVE

MEAT AND RICE

A VARIETY OF DIFFERENT
MEATS WITH MOUTHWATERING
MARINADES AND SAUCES TO
REALLY BRING OUT
THE FLAVOUR.

BEEF STROGANOFF

Trim the steak and cut into thin strips about 5 cm/2 in long.

Heat the butter and oil in a skillet and cook the onion for about 4 minutes over a low heat until translucent. Add the chopped scallions, retaining a few rings of green for final garnish.

Meanwhile mix the flour with the paprika and seasoning and coat the meat strips evenly.

And the sliced mushrooms to the onions and sauté gently for another 2 minutes. Remove the onions and mushrooms with a slotted spoon, leaving as much fat behind as possible.

Put the rice on to cook by the absorption method. Heat serving dishes and plates.

Over a fairly high heat fry the meat for a few minutes; less for fillet steak than for rump. Heat the brandy in a ladle and ignite it with a match.

Pour over the steak and allow to flame. Remove the meat and mix with the onion and mushrooms.

Add the madeira or sherry and any excess flour and paprika left over to the pan and stir well. Gradually add the broth, scraping all meat juices from the bottom of the pan. Add the meat, mushrooms and onions to the sauce and reheat for about 2–3 minutes. Turn the heat low. Add 2–3 tablespoons of sour cream and mix well.

Serve in a ring of rice garnished with parsley, sour cream, onion rings and a sprinkling of paprika. A crisp green salad or crisply cooked green vegetable, such as snowpeas or french beans, makes an excellent accompaniment to this luxurious but quickly prepared dish.

INGREDIENTS

350 g/¾ lb fillet or rump steak

25 g/1 oz butter

2 Tbsp vegetable oil

1 small onion, peeled and minced

3 scallions, washed

1 Tbsp flour

¼ tsp paprika

salt and freshly ground pepper

220 g/8 oz mushrooms, washed and sliced

1 Tbsp brandy

2 Tbsp madeira or sherry

½ cup/150 ml/¼ pt beef broth

4 Tbsp sour cream

Garnish

1 Tbsp chopped parsley

¼ tsp paprika

2 cups/220–275 g/8–10 oz long-grain rice

SPICY LAMB RISSOLES

This is an excellent dish for using up left-over lamb from a joint. These rissoles are also well suited to being made in advance and frozen until needed.

Heat the oil in a skillet and cook the minced onion for 4 minutes. Push to one side of the skillet and fry the lamb, separating the meat with a fork or a spoon.

Mix the oregano, garlic, lemon juice and cooked rice and allow to cool in a mixing bowl.

Mix together the eggs with 2 table-spoons water.

Add the seasoning, cumin, paprika and parsley to the lamb mixture and mix well. Add a little beaten egg to bind the mixture together.

With floured hands form rice and lamb mixture into 5 cm/2 in rissole shapes. Dip into the remaining egg and then into the breadcrumbs. Arrange on a tray and chill for at least 15 minutes before frying.

Heat the oil in a deep fat pan and fry for 4–5 minutes.

Serve hot with a spicy sauce and a crisp green salad.

INGREDIENTS

220 g/8 oz minced lamb
2 Tbsp vegetable oil
1 large onion, peeled and minced
½ tsp oregano
1 clove garlic, crushed
1 Tbsp lemon juice
2 cups/220 g/8 oz cooked long-grain rice
2 eggs, beaten
salt and freshly ground pepper
¼ tsp ground cumin
½ tsp paprika
1 Tbsp chopped fresh parsley
1 Tbsp flour
1 cup/110 g/4 oz dried breadcrumbs
oil for frying
1½ cups/300 ml/½ pt Spicy Tomato Sauce
(see page 153)

INGREDIENTS

700 g/1½ lb chuck steak

1¼ cups/275 ml/½ pt Coconut Milk

1 tsp brown sugar

1 Tbsp soy sauce

1 Tbsp mixed chopped nuts

2 cloves garlic, crushed

1 onion, peeled

2.5 cm/1 in fresh root ginger

2 fresh chili peppers, seeded

salt and freshly ground pepper

juice of ½ lemon

1 Tbsp cornstarch

450 g/1 lb frozen spinach or 2 lb fresh

spinach

4 Tbsp yogurt

THAI BEEF WITH SPINACH

Trim off excess fat from the meat, and cut into thin strips.

Put the coconut milk, sugar, nuts and soy sauce into a saucepan. Mix the beef with these ingredients and bring to a boil. Immediately the mixture bubbles, turn the heat down and allow to simmer for about 10 minutes.

In a blender or food processor make a paste with the garlic, onion, fresh ginger, chili peppers, a little salt and lemon juice. Mix this paste with the cornstarch and a little cold water. Add some of the hot liquid from the beef to the mixture before stirring into the beef. Cover and simmer gently for about 30–40 minutes until meat is cooked.

Cook the spinach as directed on the packet if using frozen. For fresh spinach wash and remove large stems and cook in a small amount of boiling salted water for about 5 minutes. Drain cooking water into a bowl and use to adjust sauce if it has reduced too much. Arrange drained spinach in a hot serving dish.

Put beef onto the spinach and trickle yogurt on top.

Serve with plain boiled rice.

RISOTTO WITH MEATBALLS AND CILANTRO

SERVES 4

The spicy meatballs are cooked separately from the main risotto in this recipe and served on top of the rice.

Place the ground lamb, onion, garlic, celery, cumin, cilantro, apricots, seasoning and honey in a mixing bowl and bring together. Roll into eight equal-sized balls and reserve.

Meanwhile, pour the lamb stock into a saucepan and bring to the boil. Reduce the heat to a gentle simmer.

Melt the butter in a large frying pan and gently cook the onion and garlic for 2 minutes until the onion has softened but not browned. Stir in the rice and cook for a further 2 minutes until the rice is well coated in butter.

Add a ladleful of stock to the rice and cook, stirring, until the liquid is absorbed. Continue adding the stock in small quantities until half of the stock has been used and the rice is creamy. Season well and add the coriander seeds.

Continue adding the stock until the risotto is thick but not sticky, about 25 minutes.

Meanwhile, melt the butter for the meatballs in a separate pan with the oil and cook the meatballs for 10 to 15 minutes, turning, until browned and cooked through. Drain and reserve.

Stir the cilantro into the risotto. Arrange the meatballs on top and serve.

INGREDIENTS

For the meatballs

225 g/8 oz minced lamb

1 onion, finely chopped

1 garlic clove, crushed

1 celery stalk, finely chopped

1 tsp ground cumin

1 tsp ground cilantro

3 finely chopped dried apricots

salt and ground black pepper

1 Tbsp clear honey

12 g/½ oz butter

1 Tbsp oil

For the risotto

1.1 1/2 pt lamb stock

50 g/12 oz butter

1 onion, finely chopped

2 garlic cloves, crushed

400 g/14 oz arborio rice

salt and ground black pepper

1 tsp coriander seeds, crushed

4 Tbsp chopped fresh cilantro

137

Sweet Chili and Basil Risotto

SERVES 4

Basil has a unique flavor which is closely related to its fragrance. Its oil is volatile and is lost in cooking, therefore it should only be added at the end of a recipe for full flavor.

Pour the stock into a saucepan and bring to the boil. Reduce the heat to a gentle simmer.

Meanwhile, melt the butter in a large frying pan with the oil and gently cook the beef for 2 to 3 minutes until sealed. Stir in the garlic, ginger, chili powder, soy and chili sauces and honey. Stir in the rice and cook for 2 minutes, stirring, until the rice is well coated in butter.

Add a ladleful of stock to the rice and cook, stirring, until the liquid has been absorbed. Continue to add small quantities of stock to the rice until half of the stock has been used and the rice is creamy. Season with pepper and add the red chilies, mixing well.

Continue adding the stock until the risotto becomes thick but not sticky, about 25 minutes. Just before serving, stir in the scallions and basil. Serve in a warm bowl.

INGREDIENTS

1.1 1/2 pts stock

50 g/2 oz butter

1 Tbsp oil

225 g/8 oz lean beef, trimmed and cut into strips

2 garlic cloves, crushed

2 tsp fresh ginger, chopped

1 tsp chili powder

1 Tbsp dark soy sauce

1 tsp chilli sauce

2 Tbsp clear honey

400 g/14 oz arborio rice

ground black pepper

2 red chilies, seeded and sliced

4 scallions, trimmed and sliced

4 Tbsp chopped fresh basil

Lamb Tikka with Pilau Rice and Chili Sauce

Leg of lamb sliced about 1 cm/½ in thick is best for this dish. Remove any bone or gristle. Cut into 1 cm/½-in thick cubes.

Mix yogurt with all other marinade ingredients in a plastic bag or a flat dish. Add the meat to the marinade and allow to soak for several hours. Turn from time to time.

Divide the meat onto 4 skewers and cook under a hot broiler, turning every two minutes.

Serve each portion off the skewer with pilau rice and a green salad. Garnish and, if you like, add some chilli sauce.

Ingredients

560 g/1¼ lb leg of lamb (cut in a thick slice)
¼ cup/150 ml/¼ pt natural yogurt
1 tsp chili powder
1 tsp crushed coriander
1 tsp garam masala
½ tsp salt
juice of 1 fresh lime or lemon
2 cups/220 g/8 oz pilau rice

Garnish

8 lettuce leaves
2 tomatoes, sliced
12 slices of cucumber
1 small onion, peeled and finely sliced
1 lemon or lime, quartered

Osso Buco

Heat the oil and butter in a heavy saucepan. Add the onion and garlic and cook for 3–4 minutes on a fairly low heat without browning. Remove onto a plate.

Brown the veal on all sides on a medium heat.

Add white wine and broth. Allow to cook for a few minutes. Either add the onion to the saucepan, standing the veal upright to prevent the marrow coming out of the bone, or transfer all ingredients into an ovenproof casserole in the same way.

Add chopped tomatoes and simmer on top of the cooker or in the oven for about 1 hour or until the meat is tender. Add a few drops of lemon juice to the veal.

Mix the grated rind of a lemon with the chopped parsley and sprinkle over the Osso Buco. Serve with rice. Oven temperature 180°C/350°F

Ingredients

2 Tbsp vegetable oil

50 g/2 oz butter

1 onion, peeled and sliced

1 clove garlic, crushed

900 g/2 lb shin of veal with bone

1 cup/150 ml/¼ pt white wine

1 cup/275 ml/½ pt chicken or veal broth

450 g/1 lb tomatoes or 425 g/15 oz can peeled tomatoes

1 lemon, rind and juice

1–2 tbsp fresh parsley

INGREDIENTS

300 g/11 oz pork loin

5 cups/1.2 l water

2 Tbsp tomato paste

3 Tbsp light soy sauce

3 Tbsp sugar

3 drops of red food coloring (optional)

1½ Tbsp cornstarch

3 cups/350 g/12 oz cooked rice, heated

Nam Chim Sauce

4 Tbsp white vinegar

2 Tbsp dark soya sauce

1 fresh red chili, sliced thinly

¼ tsp sugar

RED PORK WITH RICE

The red-colored marinade soaks a little way into the meat from the surface; when sliced, the red edges of the pork make this a decorative as well as a tasty dish.

Mix together the pork, water, tomato paste, soy sauce, sugar and food colouring in a bowl and leave to marinate for 1 hour.

Put the pork mixture with its marinade in a pan, bring to a boil and simmer for 30 minutes. Remove the pork and place in an ovenproof dish; roast it in a preheated 180°C/350°F oven for 10 minutes until lightly browned and glazed. Reserve the cooking liquid.

Mix a little of the cooking liquid with the cornstarch and then stir in ½ cup/450 ml/16 floz more liquid. Bring to a boil in a small pan to thicken, then remove from the heat.

Mix together the ingredients for the nam chim sauce. Sauté the pork and place on serving plates (on top of the hot rice). Spoon the cornstarchsauce over the top, and serve with nam chim sauce on the side.

Serve accompanied by sliced cucumber, scallions, hard-cooked eggs and pieces of deep-fried fresh pork fat back or pork belly.

MARINATED LAMB CHOPS
WITH SAVORY RICE

Place the chops in a plastic bag with the mixed marinade. Allow to soak for several hours. Turn the bag around on a dish to help the meat to contact the marinade.

Arrange the chops on a rack over a roasting pan and place in a preheated oven. Cook for 15–20 minutes.

Make the sauce by adding 1 tablespoon oil to a saucepan and cooking the minced onion for 3 minutes. Add the sherry, water, redcurrant jelly, coriander, seasoning and pineapple pieces. Simmer for 15 minutes. The sauce may be blended before serving. Alternatively mix 1 teaspoon cornstarch with 1 tablespoon water, add a little warmed sauce and return to the saucepan. Stir until sauce is slightly thickened.

Lay the chops on a bed of savory rice, sprinkled with chopped parsley. Pour sauce as you like. Oven temperature 200°C/400°F

INGREDIENTS

8 best end of neck chops

Marinade

2 Tbsp oil

2 Tbsp soy sauce

1 tsp brown sugar

salt and freshly ground pepper

1 tsp lemon juice

Sauce

1 onion, peeled

2 Tbsp sherry

2 Tbsp water

2 Tbsp redcurrant jelly

¼ Tbsp ground coriander

100 g/4 oz canned pineapple pieces

1 Tbsp fresh parsley

2 cups/220 g/8 oz savoury rice

oven temperature 200°C/400°F

MADRAS BEEF CURRY

Heat 4 tablespoons oil in a skillet. Cut off a few thin onion rings for garnish, and then mince the remainder and cook for 5 minutes.

Remove the strings from the celery and mince. Add to the onions and stir well for a further 2 minutes. Remove to a casserole or heavy-based saucepan.

Trim the steak and remove any gristle. Cut into 2.5 cm/1-in cubes. Sprinkle with flour, seasoned with the paprika and garam masala. Add remaining oil to the frying pan and fry the meat until golden on all sides. Remove with a slotted spoon to the casserole.

Sprinkle the curry powder and any remaining flour into the pan and simmer for 2 minutes. Add the tomato paste to the broth and pour into the pan, stirring well to remove meat juices. Add the canned tomatoes and bring to the boil.

Meanwhile cut the potato into cubes and bring to a boil for 5 minutes in salted water.

Add the tomato and curry mixture to the meat and onions. Stir well.

Drain the potato cubes and add to the casserole with ½ teaspoon salt. Cook in the oven for 1 hour or until the meat is tender. Taste and season accordingly.

Serve with pilau rice, mango chutney and poppadoms or any of the other side dishes or sambals which are so popular with curry.

VARIATION

This curry can be cooked on top of the cooker but remember to check from time to time that it is not sticking or drying out. Add a little broth or water if necessary. Oven temperature 350°F.

INGREDIENTS

6 Tbsp vegetable oil

2 large onions, peeled

4 stalks celery, washed

700 g/1½ lb chuck stuck

1 Tbsp flour

½ tsp paprika

½ tsp garam masala

1–2 Tbsp Madras curry powder

1 bay leaf

1 tsp tomato paste

1½ cups/570 ml/1 pt beef broth or water

425 g/15 oz can peeled tomatoes

1 medium potato, peeled

Garnish

1 Tbsp chopped fresh parsley

MIXED MEAT RISOTTO

SERVES 4

This recipe uses one of the best known Italian ingredients, prosciutto. It has a delicate flavor and is perfect with the pork and garlic flavored mortadella sausage.

Pour the stock and wine into a pan and bring to the boil. Reduce the heat to a gentle simmer.

Meanwhlle, melt the butter in a large skillet and gently cook the pork for 2 minutes until sealed. Add the onion and garlic and cook, stirring, until the onion has softened but not browned. Stir in the rice and cook for 2 minutes, stirring, until the rice is coated in butter.

Add a ladleful of stock and cook gently until the liquid has been absorbed. Continue to add small quantities of stock until half of the stock has been used and the rice is creamy. Season well.

Continue adding the stock for 20 minutes. Stir in the prosciutto and mortadella, sun-dried tomatoes and basil. Cook for a further 5 minutes until the risotto is thick but not sticky.

Just before serving, stir in the cheese and serve in a warmed bowl.

INGREDIENTS

3¾ cups/900 ml/1½ pts vegetable or pork stock

1⅓ cups/300 ml/½ pt dry white wine

50 g/2 oz butter

150 g/5 oz lean pork, trimmed and cubed

1 onion, finely chopped

2 garlic cloves, sliced

400 g/14 oz arborio rice

salt and ground black pepper

50 g/2 oz prosciutto, cut into strips

175 g/6 oz quartered mortadella slices

12 sun-dried tomatoes in oil, drained and cut into strips

2 Tbsp chopped fresh basil

2 Tbsp freshly grated Parmesan cheese

BEEF SATÉ

Place all the main ingredients except the meat in a blender to make a paste.

Trim the meat and cut into small squares. Mix with the paste and allow to marinate for several hours.

Arrange the meat on skewers.

Make the sauce by mixing all the sauce ingredients except the lemon juice together in a saucepan. Bring to a boil and simmer for about 20 minutes. Add the lemon juice.

While the sauce is cooking turn the broiler onto a high heat and allow the skewered meat to cook. Turn every 2 minutes for the first 6 minutes, then lower the heat and continue cooking. The time will depend on whether you like your meat slightly rare or well cooked.

Accompany with boiled rice.

INGREDIENTS

2 scallions, washed

2.4 cm/1 in fresh root ginger, shredded

2 cloves garlic, crushed

8 cardamom pods

1 tsp cumin seeds

1 tsp coriander seeds

juice of 1 lemon

1 tsp shredded or ground nutmeg

2 bay leaves

2 Tbsp oil

700 g/1½ lb rump steak

Saté Sauce

6 Tbsp peanut butter

1 Tbsp brown sugar

2 chii peppers, seeded

1 tsp sugar

juice and rind of 1 lemon

½ cup/150 ml/¼ pt beef broth

2 cups/220 g/8 oz long-grain rice, cooked

BEEFBURGERS WITH SPICY TOMATO SAUCE

Place the meat in a bowl with the very minced onion.

Chop the bell pepper into very small dice. If you prefer, both onion and bell pepper can be chopped in a blender.

Add the breadcrumbs. Mix with a beaten egg and add the Worcestershire sauce and seasoning.

Divide the mixture into 8 pieces and shape into rounds. A scone or pastry cutter is ideal for this purpose. Place on a tray in the refrigerator to chill while making the sauce.

To make the sauce heat the oil in a saucepan and cook over a low heat for 4 minutes. Add the garlic and shredded carrot. Stir well and then add remaining ingredients. Season well. Simmer for at least 20 minutes on a low heat.

Brush the beefburgers over with oil and broil under a high heat for 4 minutes each side. If you like beef well cooked give the burgers a further 3 minutes.

INGREDIENTS

450 g/1 lb lean minced beef

1 onion, peeled and minced

1 green bell pepper, seeded

2 Tbsp fresh breadcrumbs

1 egg

1 tsp Worcestershire sauce

salt and freshly ground pepper

Spicy Tomato Sauce

1 tsp oil

1 onion, peeled and minced

1 chili pepper seeded (optional)

1 clove garlic, minced

1 carrot, scraped and shredded

200 g/7 oz can peeled tomatoes

½ cup/150 ml/¼ pt broth or water

1 bay leaf

½ tsp oregano

2 cups/220 g/8 oz long-grain rice

LAMB'S LIVER WITH CREAM SAUCE

Slice the liver into even sized pieces. Dip each piece into the seasoned flour until it is evenly coated.

Heat the butter and oil in a frying pan on a low heat. Cook the sliced onion for 4 minutes until transparent and then transfer to a casserole. Sprinkle the remaining seasoned flour into the casserole and stir around.

Carefully fry each slice of liver in the remaining fat for 1 minute on each side.

Transfer the liver into the casserole. Add the sherry, broth and tomatoes to the frying pan and bring to the boil. Pour over the liver and cook for about 30 minutes.

Serve on a heated dish with a border of boiled rice, sprinkled with chopped parsley. Oven temperature 180°C/350°F

INGREDIENTS

450 g/1 lb lamb's or calf's liver

2 Tbsp seasoned flour

25 g/1 oz butter

2–3 Tbsp vegetable oil

1 large onion, sliced

1 clove garlic, minced (optional)

2–3 Tbsp medium sherry

½ cup broth

7 oz can/200 g/7 oz peeled tomatoes, sliced

salt and freshly ground black pepper

3 Tbsp whipping cream

2 cups/220–275 g/8–10 oz boiled rice

Garnish

1 Tbsp freshly chopped parsley

INGREDIENTS

1 roasted duck (rub with red food coloring before roasting), boned and cut into
6 x 1 cm/2½ x ½ in slices
7 cups/750 g/1¾ lb cooked rice
4 Tbsp thinly sliced pickled ginger
4 Tbsp thinly sliced sweet dill or pickled cucumber

Cooked Sauce

2 cups/450 ml/16 floz chicken broth
1 Tbsp sugar
½ Tbsp light soya sauce
¼ Tbsp dark soya sauce
1 tsp flour

Soya Chilli Rice

6 tbsp/75 ml/3 floz dark soy sauce
3 fresh red chillies, sliced thinly into circles
1 Tbsp sugar
½ Tbsp vinegar

DUCK WITH RICE

A very popular dish, of Chinese origin, with two contrasting sauces.

Heat the ingredients for the cooked sauce together in a pan and boil for 1 minute. Mix the ingredients for the raw sauce in a bowl and put to one side.

Warm the duck and rice in a preheated 350°F oven for 5 minutes. Then, divide the rice between 4 serving plates, and arrange the duck meat over the top. Spoon the cooked sauce on top of each, and place ginger and pickle slices around the edges. Serve with the raw sauce on the side.

Souvlakia with Rice

Ingredients

450 g/1 lb leg of lamb

12 bay leaves

juice of ½ a lemon

2 Tbsp olive oil

salt and freshly ground pepper

1 tsp oregano

2 cups/220–275 g/8–10 oz long-grain rice, cooked

This dish is delicious when cooked on a barbecue.

Use one skewer for each person. Cut the lamb into 2 cm/1-in cubes and thread onto the skewers with pieces of bay leaf in between. Leave space at either end of the skewers to enable them to rest on the broiler pan.

Beat the lemon juice into the olive oil, season with salt, pepper and oregano and leave the lamb to marinate in the mixture in a plastic bag for at least 1 hour.

Cook under a hot broiler for about 10 minutes turning occasionally, so that the lamb becomes well seared on the outside and tender and juicy inside.

Serve immediately with a tomato and cucumber salad, quarters of lemon to squeeze over the meat and a dish of cooked rice. Serve lemon juice or seasoned yogurt on all types of accompanying salads.

157

BEEF RAGOUT RISOTTO

SERVES 4

A ragout is a thick, spiced stew of meat, fish or poultry that can be made with or without vegetables. This recipe combines classic flavors to make a deliciously satisfying meal.

Pour the stock and wine into a saucepan and bring to the boil. Reduce the heat to a gentle simmer.

Meanwhile melt the butter in a large skillet with the oil and gently fry the beef for 3 minutes, stirring, until sealed. Add the onion and garlic and cook for 2 minutes until the onion is softened but not browned. Stir in the rice and cook,

stirring, for 2 minutes until the rice is well coated in butter.

Add a ladleful of the stock and wine mixture to the rice and cook gently, stirring, until the liquid is absorbed. Continue adding small quantities of the stock mixture until half of the stock has been used and the rice is creamy. Season well and add the carrot, celery, tomato purée, and tomatoes.

Continue adding the stock mixture until the risotto becomes thick but not sticky, about 25 minutes. Sprinkle in the herbs and serve in a warm bowl with warm crusty bread.

INGREDIENTS

3¾ cups/900 ml/1½ pts beef stock

1⅓ cups/300 ml/½ pt red wine

50 g/2 oz butter

1 tsp oil

225 g/8 oz lean beef, trimmed and cubed

1 large onion, cut into eight

1 garlic clove, crushed

100 g/1 1 oz arborio rice

salt and ground black pepper

1 carrot, halved and sliced

2 celery sticks, sliced

1 Tbsp tomato purée

2 large tomatoes, seeded and chopped

1 Tbsp chopped fresh oregano

159

CHAPTER SIX

NOODLES WITH TOPPINGS

AN ARRAY OF INTERESTING

TOPPINGS TO TURN ORDINARY

NOODLES INTO SOMETHING

REALLY SPECIAL.

FRIED EGG NOODLES WITH PORK AND EGGPLANT SAUCE

INGREDIENTS

400 g/14 oz fresh or 275 g/10 oz dried
medium egg noodles

2 Tbsp sesame oil

Sauce

275 g/10 oz boneless belly of pork, skinned
and thinly sliced

2½ tbsp light soy sauce

2½ Tbsp Chinese rice wine or dry sherry

4 Tbsp cornstarch

4 Tbsp vegetable oil

2.5 cm/1 in fresh ginger, peeled and finely
chopped

2 cloves garlic, finely chopped

300 g/11 oz eggplant, sliced into bite-sized
pieces and soaked in water

100 g/4 oz carrots, sliced

16 tinned straw mushrooms, halved

2 scallions, chopped into 2.5 cm/1 in lengths

black bell pepper

2½ cups/570 ml/1 pt chicken broth

2 Tbsp oyster sauce

1 tsp superfine sugar

4 tbsp water

Oyster sauce is a frequently used Chinese flavoring. The surprising thing about oyster sauce is that you would be hard put to find any trace of fishiness in its flavor. It will last for long periods if kept refrigerated and is widely available from supermarkets.

Marinate the pork in 1 tablespoon each of soy sauce, rice wine and cornstarch. Set aside for 30 minutes, then heat 1 tablespoon of the vegetable oil in a wok or frying pan and fry the pork for about 3 minutes until lightly browned. Clean the wok.

Heat the rest of the vegetable oil in the work until very hot and stir fry the ginger and garlic for 30 seconds. Add the drained aubergine and carrots and stir-fry for a further 1–2 minutes. Add the pork, mushrooms and scallions, sprinkle over the black bell pepper and stir.

Add the chicken broth, rice wine, oyster sauce, soy sauce and sugar and bring to a boil, simmering for 1 minute. Dissolve the cornstarch in the water and add to thicken the sauce.

Boil the egg noodles in plenty of water for 4 minutes. Rinse under running water and drain. Heat the sesame oil in a wok, add the noodles and quickly stir-fry.

Divide the egg noodles onto four plates, pour the pork and eggplant sauce over, then serve at once.

Ingredients

200 g/7 oz dried thin egg noodles
vegetable oil for deep frying

Filling

6 Tbsp vegetable oil
450 g/1 lb boneless chicken breasts, sliced diagonally into bite-sized pieces
salt and black bell pepper
3 Tbsp cornstarch
4 cloves garlic, finely chopped
4 cm/1½ in fresh ginger, peeled and finely chopped
100 g/4 oz can bamboo shoots, sliced into matchsticks
⅔ red bell pepper, diced
4 scallions, chopped

Sauce

150 ml/¼ cup chicken broth (see page 12)
1 Tbsp Chinese rice wine or dry sherry
1 Tbsp light soy sauce
2 tsp dark soy sauce
4 tsp tomato ketchup
½ tsp superfine sugar
salt and black bell pepper
½ Tbsp cornstarch
2 tsp water

Chicken and Red Bell Pepper in Egg Noodle

Noodle baskets are a Chinese innovation that appeal as much to the eyes as to the taste buds. You will need two small sieves about 12 cm/5 in across. I find this recipe works best with thinner noodles, and the oil needs to be hot to get nice crisp golden baskets. This recipe makes six baskets which can be presented as a main dish or as a starter with less filling.

Boil the egg noodles for 3 minutes. Rinse with water, drain, separate and dry on a tray lined with paper towel.

Heat the oil in a deep pan. Oil the strainers, one on the inside, the other on the outside. Line one strain with egg noodles and press down lightly the other sieve to sandwich them. Carefully deep fry the noodles with the two strainers holding them together until crispy and golden, about 3–4 minutes. Remove the noodle basket, taking care not to break it. Create 5 more baskets in the same way.

Heat 4 tablespoons of oil in a wok or frying pan. Sprinkle the chicken with the salt and bell pepper, then coat with the cornstarch. Shallow fry the chicken for 3–4 minutes or until golden brown. Drain on absorbent paper.

Heat the remaining 2 tablespoons of oil in the work, stir-fry the garlic and ginger, then add the bamboo, red bell pepper and onion. Stir well. Add the chicken broth, rice wine, soy sauce, ketchup and superfine sugar, bring to the boil and season if required.

Combine the cornstarch and water and add to thicken the sauce. Return the chicken to the pan and stir. Place the noodle baskets on 6 plates and put the chicken in them. Serve at once.

CRISPY RICE VERMICELLI WITH SHREDDED CHICKEN

You will be surprised at the rapid expansion of the vermicelli the first time you try this dish. The key is to deep fry it in small amounts to prevent it from overflowing from your wok or pan. The noodles are ready when they have lost their transparency and have turned white.

Fill a wok or saucepan a quarter full of vegetable oil and heat. Deep fry the rice vermicelli in small batches at a time. It will puff up in seconds. Drain on absorbent paper.

Marinate the chicken in 1 tablespoon each of the soy sauce, rice wine and cornstarch for 30 minutes. Heat 2 tablespoons of oil in a wok or frying pan and fry the chicken for 3–4 minutes. Set aside and clean the wok.

Heat the remaining 2 tablespoons of the vegetable oil in the wok. Add the ginger and stir-fry for 30 seconds. Add the *shiitake* mushrooms, water chestnuts, scallions and chicken, sprinkle with salt and bell pepper, then stir-fry for 1–2 minutes.

Add the chicken broth, sesame oil, tomato ketchup, sugar and remaining soy sauce and rice wine, and bring to a boil. Combine the remaining cornstarch and water, then add to thicken the sauce. Stir well.

To serve, pile the lettuce leaves onto a small plate. Put the crispy vermicelli on to four individual plates and pour the chicken sauce over. When you eat, take one lettuce leaf and wrap some noodles and chicken sauce together in a bundle and pop into your mouth.

INGREDIENTS

100 g/4 oz rice vermicelli

vegetable oil for deep frying

Sauce

450 g/1 lb boneless chicken breasts, shredded

2 Tbsp light soy sauce

2 Tbsp Chinese rice wine or dry sherry

3 Tbsp cornstarch

4 Tbsp vegetable oil

2.5 cm1 in fresh ginger, peeled and finely chopped

8 *shiitake* mushrooms, shredded

12 water chestnuts, sliced

4 scallions, chopped into 2.5 cm/1 in lengths

salt and black bell pepper

425 ml/1¾ cups chicken broth (see page 12)

1 tsp sesame oil

1 Tbsp tomato ketchup

½ tsp sugar

3 Tbsp water

6 lettuce leaves, rinsed and quartered

CRAB MEAT SAUCE ON PAN-FRIED EGG NOODLES

Cook the egg noodles in plenty of water for 4 minutes. Rinse, drain well and divide into four. Heat 1 tablespoon of oil in a wok or frying pan until very hot. Press one portion of the egg noodles down lightly into the pan and fry until lightly browned on both sides. Place on a chopping board and cut a criss-cross pattern. Remove to a plate. Repeat with the three remaining portions.

Heat two tablespoons of oil in the cleaned wok. Fry the garlic and ginger for 30 seconds. Add the *shiitake* mushrooms, bamboo shoots and eggplants and stir-fry for 1–2 minutes. Add the crab meat, water and soy sauce and season. Bring to the boil and simmer for 1 minute.

Dissolve the cornstarch in the water and add to thicken the sauce. Stir. Pour the sauce over the noodles and serve.

INGREDIENTS

275 g/10 oz dried *or* 400 g/14 oz fresh medium egg noodles
4 Tbsp vegetable oil

Crab Meat Sauce

2 Tbsp vegetable oil
1 clove garlic, finely chopped
1 cm/½ in fresh ginger, peeled and finely chopped
10 *shiitake* mushrooms, sliced
175 g/6 oz can bamboo shoots, sliced into matchsticks
4 scallions, chopped
350 g/12 oz can crab meat
2½ cups/570 ml/1 pt water
4 tsp light soy sauce
salt and black bell pepper
3 Tbsp cornstarch
4 Tbsp water

Malaysian Egg Noodles with Chicken and Shrimps

A Malaysian Chinese dish with a characteristic savory sauce. A typical feature of Malaysian and Singaporean cookery is the frequent use of egg, as in this dish, in which strands of beaten egg are stirred into the sauce.

Boil plenty of water in a pan and add the egg noodles. Cook for 3 minutes and rinse under cold water and drain. Heat the sesame oil in a wok or frying pan and fry the noodles. Then divide onto four plates.

Heat the vegetable oil in a wok or frying pan until very hot. Fry the garlic for 30 seconds. Add the chicken and fry for 2–3 minutes. Add the shrimps and stir, then add the fish balls, bean sprouts and spinach or greens, stirring for 2–3 minutes.

Add the soy sauce, salt, bell pepper, sugar and chicken broth; bring to the boil. Dissolve the cornstarch in water, then add to thicken the sauce. When the sauce returns to a boil, stir in the beaten egg and wait for the egg strands to float up to the surface. Pour the sauce over the noodles and serve.

Ingredients

1¾ cups/400 g/4 oz fresh *or* 275 g/10 oz dried thin egg noodles

2 Tbsp sesame oil

4 Tbsp vegetable oil

2 cloves garlic, finely chooped

100 g/4 oz boneless chicken breasts, sliced into bite-sized pieces

¾ cup/100 g/4 oz peeled shrimps

4 fish balls, sliced

1 cup/220 g/8 oz bean sprouts

½ cup/100 g/4 oz mustard greens *or* fresh spinach

1 tsp light soy sauce

1 tsp salt

white bell pepper

½ tsp superfine sugar

2½ cups/570 ml/1 pt chicken broth (see page 12)

3 Tbsp cornstarch

4 Tbsp water

2 eggs, beaten

CRISPY EGG NOODLES WITH PORK SAUCE

Deep-fried noodles might seem like a strange idea, but, in fact, are very popular throughout Asia, and make a crunchy and refreshing alternative to boiled noodles.

Boil plenty of water in a saucepan and cook the noodles for 3 minutes. Rinse and drain. Separate and spread the noodles on a tray to dry.

Heat a wok or saucepan a quarter full of oil and heat to. Deep fry the egg noodles in small batches until golden and crispy. Drain on absorbent paper.

Put the pork, soy sauce and 1 tablespoon of the cornstarch in a bowl, mix and leave for 15 minutes. Soak the *shiitake* mushrooms in 1 cup hot water for 15 minutes, then remove and quarter. Retain the water. Heat 2 tablespoons of the oil in a wok or frying pan and fry the pork for about 3 minutes. Set aside and clean the pan.

Heat the remaining oil in the wok and fry the ginger and garlic for 30 seconds, before adding the carrots, *shiitake* mushrooms and Chinese cabbages. Stir-fry for 2–3 minutes. Add the meat and season with salt and bell pepper and stir.

Add the water used to soak the mushrooms, chicken broth, rice wine and sugar and bring to a boil. Check the saltiness. Dissolve the cornstarch in the water and add to thicken the sauce. Crush the crispy noodles lightly then put onto four plates. Pour the sauce over and serve at once.

INGREDIENTS

1 cup/220 g/8 oz dried thin egg noodles
vegetable oil for deep frying

Sauce

220g/8 oz lean pork, sliced on the slant into bite-sized pieces
1 tbsp light soy sauce
4 Tbsp cornstarch
8 large dried *shiitake* mushrooms, rinsed
4 Tbsp vegetable oil
1 in fresh ginger, peeled and finely chopped
2 cloves garlic, finely chopped
1 medium-sized onion, cut into bite-sized squares
100 g/4 oz carrots, thinly sliced
1 cup/220 g/8 oz Chinese cabbage, cut into bite-sized squares
salt and black bell pepper
2½ cups/570 ml/1 pt chicken broth
(see page 12)
2 Tbsp Chinese rice wine or dry sherry
2 tsp superfine sugar
4 Tbsp water

Soft Egg Noodles with Minced Pork Sauce

Toban djan *is a fiery Chinese chili bean sauce available from most Chinese or Oriental stores and in a growing number of supermarkets. Here, the power of the chili sauce is tempered by the addition of yellow bean sauce leaving the dish pleasantly spicy rather than breathtakingly hot.*

Cook the egg noodles in plenty of boiling water for 3 minutes. Rinse and drain. Toss in the sesame oil and divide into four servings.

Heat the vegetable oil in a pan and stir-fry the garlic, ginger and scallions for 30 seconds. Add the minced pork and fry for 3–4 minutes. Add the yellow bean sauce, chili sauce, rice wine and soy sauce and stir for one minute.

Add the mixture of broth and cornstarch and stir until the sauce thickens. Season with salt and black bell pepper to taste. Pour the sauce over the noodles and serve immediately.

Ingredients

1¼ cups/275 g/10 oz dried *or* 400 g/14 oz fresh thin egg noodles

2 tsp sesame oil

Sauce

2 Tbsp vegetable oil

1 large clove garlic, finely chopped

1 cm/½ in fresh ginger, peeled and finely chopped

2 scallions, chopped

450 g/1 lb minced pork

3 Tbsp yellow bean sauce

1 Tbsp chili bean sauce (*toban djan*)

2 Tbsp Chinese rice wine or dry sherry

2 Tbsp dark soy sauce

1¾ cups/450 ml/¾ pt chicken broth (see page 12) mixed to a paste with 2 tbsp cornstarch

salt and black bell pepper

CHAPTER SEVEN

DESSERTS

FUN IDEAS FOR SOME UNUSUAL

AND DELICIOUS DESSERTS.

MAKING THE RICE PUDDING

INGREDIENTS

1 Creamy Rice Pudding (see below)

2 Tbsp soft brown sugar

4 slices canned pineapple, drained

4 glacé cherries

Creamy Rice Pudding

25 g/1 oz butter

50 g/2 oz short-grain rice

1 cup/300 ml/½ pt evapourated milk

½ cup/25 g/1 oz sugar

½ tsp ground nutmeg

Butter an ovenproof pie dish.

Wash the rice several times in a sieve with running cold water. Drain

Pour the evapourated milk and water into the pie dish and sprinkle the rice on top. Add the sugar and stir well. If time allows leave to stand in the refrigerator for 1-2 hours as this improves the pudding.

Sprinkle with nutmeg and add a few small pieces of butter to the surface.

Bake in the oven for 30-40 minutes on a low shelf, then stir well to separate the grains. Continue cooking for a further 1-1¼ hours.

This will produce a rice pudding with a skin on top which many people enjoy. If no skin is wanted cover with loose foil. Oven temperature 150°C/300°F

PINEAPPLE RICE PUDDING

Make the Rice Pudding and cook covered in foil to prevent a skin forming.

Remove the foil after 1¼ hours and sprinkle with the brown sugar and arrange the pineapple rings on top.

Return to the oven for a further 30–40 minutes.

Decorate with glacé cherries in the center of each pineapple ring.

Rice Soufflé Pudding

Ingredients

1 cup/100 g/4 oz short-grain rice

½ cup/75 g/3 oz sugar

50 g/2 oz butter

3¾ cups/850 ml/1½ pt milk

4 eggs, separated

1 vanilla pod or a few drops of vanilla extract

Sauce

1¼ cups/275 ml/½ pt blended pineapple

2 tsp cornstarch

2 Tbsp water

Rinse the rice well several times in cold water and allow to drain in the strainer. Sprinkle the rice into a pan of hot water. Bring to a boil and cook for 3 minutes. Drain and pour boiling water from the kettle over the grains.

Add the sugar and half the butter to most of the milk, keeping some to mix with the egg yolks. Add the vanilla pod at this stage but if you are using vanilla extract add it at the end of the cooking. Heat the mixture and add the rice. Cook until tender for about 30 minutes. After 15 minutes add a little of the hot rice to the egg yolks and milk and then return to the rice. Stir well for the remainder of the cooking time. Allow to cool slightly.

Butter a 17.5 cm/7-in soufflé dish. Preheat the oven. Put 1 cm/½ in water in the bottom of a roasting pan.

Whip up the egg whites to a fluffy consistency but do not over-beat. Fold the vanilla extract and egg whites into the rice mixture and turn into a soufflé dish standing in the water. Cook for 25–30 minutes.

For a sauce any blended fruit or fruit juice will do. Mix the cornstarch with the water and add to the blended fruit. Heat over a low heat until slightly thickened.

This soufflé should be served straight from the oven. Oven temperature 190°C/375°F

RICE EGGS WITH PEACH SAUCE

INGREDIENTS

½ cup/75 g/3 oz short-grain rice

½ cup/50 g/2 oz sugar

3 egg yolks

2½ cups/275 ml/½ pt milk

½ tsp vanilla extract

1 Tbsp golden raisins

1 Tbsp mixed nuts, chopped

To coat

1 egg

1 cup dried breadcrumbs

To fry

3¾ cups/1 1/1¾ pt vegetable oil

Peach Sauce

1 small can of peaches

2 tsp arrowroot

Wash the rice several times in cold water. Bring to a boil in a pan of water and boil for 10 minutes. Drain into a strainer.

Cook the rice and milk in a saucepan until the rice is soft. Stir over a low heat to prevent sticking.

Add sugar and vanilla and stir until the mixture leaves the sides of the pan. Turn out onto a plate. Chill.

Divide into pieces about the size of a small egg and roll on a floured board.

Dip the croquettes in egg and bread-crumbs and deep fry in the vegetable oil until golden brown.

To make the peach sauce, strain or blend the fruit.

Mix the arrowroot with a little cold water and stir into the fruit mixture.

Heat over a low heat until thickened and serve with the croquettes.

Sprinkle with golden raisins and mixed nuts and serve with cream, custard or a fruit purée sauce.

INGREDIENTS

1½ cups/175 g/6 oz all-purpose flour

½ cup/75 g/3 oz ground rice

220 g/8 oz butter

½ cup/110 g/4 oz sugar

a pinch of salt

SHORTBREAD
MAKES 2 CAKES

Sift the flour and ground rice into a bowl.

Making sure the butter is fairly soft, place it in another bowl and add the sugar. Squeeze the sugar and butter together by hand so they mix well but it is not necessary to cream the mixture.

Add the salt to the flour and then gradually work in the lump of butter and sugar until a smooth ball is formed.

Turn out onto a floured surface which is a mixture of ground rice and flour. Knead until smooth. Roll out 2 balls, shape in a thistle mold. If a shortbread mold is not available cook two cakes in 15 cm/6 in flan rings or sandwich pans. Mark the edges.

Cook in the oven for 1 hour.

Sprinkle with sugar when cooling. Oven temperature 170°C/325°F

MANGO AND KIWI HEDGEHOG

2 ripe mangos

2 ripe kiwi fruits

400 g/14 oz can creamy rice pudding

Cut the mangos in half. Remove the stones. Run a small, sharp knife in straight lines down each half, scoring the fruit without cutting the skin.

Turn the halved, marked fruit inside out carefully.

Peel the kiwi fruits and slice. Arrange the kiwi slices in between the mango cubes.

Divide the rice into 4 portions on serving plates and top with the mango hedgehog.

RASPBERRY, PEACH, AND HAZELNUT RISOTTO

SERVES 4

This is a colorful combination of ingredients usually found in Peach Melba. Stirred into rice sweetened with peach nectar, it is sensational.

Pour the milk and cream into a saucepan with the peach nectar and bring to a boil. Reduce the heat to a gentle simmer.

Meanwhile, melt the butter in a large skillet and gently cook the nuts for 1 minute, stirring. Add the rice and cook, stirring, for a further 2 minutes until the rice is well coated in butter.

Add a ladleful of the milk, cream and nectar mixture and cook gently, stirring, until absorbed. Stir in the sugar and continue adding the liquid in small quantities for a further 20 minutes.

Stir in the peaches and raspberries, cook for 4 to 5 minutes until the risotto is thick but not sticky. Serve in a warm dish, decorated with mint.

INGREDIENTS

2½ cups/600 ml/1 pt milk

1¼ cups/300 ml/½ pt heavy cream

1¼ cups/300 ml/½ pt peach nectar

50 g/2 oz butter

50 g/2 oz coarsely chopped hazelnuts

400 g/14 oz arborio rice

12 g/½ oz icing sugar

225 g/8 oz canned or fresh peach quarters

65g/2½ oz raspberries

mint sprigs, to decorate

Ingredients

2 eggs

5 Tbsp sugar

2 tsp vanilla extract

½ tsp shgredded nutmeg

½ tsp shredded lemon peel

½ tsp salt

2 tsp baking powder

2 cups/220 g/8 oz cold cooked rice

1 cup/100 g/4 oz all purpose flour

vegetable oil for frying

confectioners sugar

Calas

MAKES ABOUT 20

These sweet rice cakes are deep-fried, sprinkled with confectioner's sugar, and served for breakfast like small pastries. They are delicious hot, and it's hard to stop with just one or two.

In a mixing bowl, combine the eggs and sugar and beat until pale yellow. Add the vanilla extract, nutmeg, lemon, salt, baking powder and rice, and mix well. Add enough flour to bind the ingredients.

In a deep frying pan or wok heat 7.5 cm/3 in oil. Drop teaspoonfuls of the batter into the oil, but do not crowd.

Fry until golden, turning once, about 4 minutes. Remove, drain briefly, place on absorbent paper towel and keep warm. Make sure the oil does not overheat before frying the next batch.

Sift confectioner's sugar over the calas, or put the sugar in a bag, add a few calas at a time, and shake.

I N D E X

Unlock Your Horse's Talent

in 20 minutes a day

A 3-step training program for
every horse

Richard Maxwell
& Johanna Sharples

David & Charles

A DAVID & CHARLES BOOK

Photography by Matthew Roberts
with the exception of the following:
Bob Atkins pp25, 29, 34, 35(left), 37, 40,
  41
Kit Houghton p105
Your Horse magazine/Angus Murray
  p27(top)

Artwork on p122 by Maggie Raynor

First published in the UK in 2003

Distributed in North America
by F&W Publications, Inc.
4700 E. Galbraith Rd.
Cincinnati, OH 45236
1-800-289-0963

A catalogue record for this book is
available from the British Library.

ISBN 0 7153 1312 6

Commissioning Editor: Jane Trollope
Art Editor: Sue Cleave
Project Editor: Jo Weeks
Production Controller: Ros Napper

Printed in Italy by Stige
for David & Charles
Brunel House Newton Abbot Devon

Contents

A Way of Life

Riding and handling horses is more a lifestyle than a sport. Most people who have anything to do with horses, including myself, spend their lives trying to absorb as much information about them as possible in the hope and belief that if they can only learn to communicate better with their horse, improve their techniques or build more confidence, they'll be that bit closer to the harmonious partnership they seek. There are a few who channel their desire for improvement in a more

> **Horses usually give you what you deserve, rather than what you expect or what you think you deserve**

material direction – if they could afford a bigger lorry, more lessons, a better-bred horse, they'd get there faster. Maybe when they've got all those things, they will realize they've been chasing a shadow because nothing changes the fundamental truth: horses usually give you what you deserve, rather than what you expect or what you think you deserve. I say *usually*, because, luckily for us all, horses tend to be very tolerant of our mistakes, and my experience is that, in fact, they give us far *more* than we deserve.

It's important to recognize that just because your horse is too generous to point out that you are wrong, it doesn't make you right! When we're caught up trying to juggle our riding with other commitments, it can be easy to get frustrated and abuse their tolerance, particularly if we set our hearts on improving our performance

without really knowing how to go about it, or if we believe we lack the time or skills to do it 'right'. I'm certainly someone who has fallen into this trap over the years, and this is partly what has led me to develop the techniques you'll find in this book.

HOW DO I DO IT RIGHT?

So, what is the 'right' way to train a horse? In my view, there isn't one, but there are certain principles that seem to hold true in any number of different situations, and particular techniques which I have found effective in almost every circumstance. I have tried to convey these principles and techniques in this book, but they are not set in stone: I am constantly learning more from the horses and people I come across every day of my life.

I advise horse owners to be very suspicious of 'gurus' and those who lay claim to having found the perfect system. All too often they think they have found the 'only' system. Such dogmatism leads to them closing their minds to other possibilities and cuts them off from the immense amount of learning to be gained from others who may be following a different route. As the saying goes: more than one road leads to Rome. Which route you choose depends on how long you want to take, where you want to visit on the way and what itinerary best suits your horse. Some people relish the challenge of getting there by the quickest but hardest way, others prefer the more scenic route. Anyone who approaches the journey with a good map and the patience to go at

the pace that suits their horse should get there eventually though! That's not to say that having low expectations of yourself and your horse is a road to success.

Performance is important to all of us, whether we want to compete or not. Who doesn't want a well-behaved, safe and reliable horse that's a pleasure to be around, and the

sooner the better? No matter what the animal's size, breed or purpose in life, all of us should expect this much as a basic minimum.

What most of us desire from our horses is performance without intimidation, obedience without dominance, fun without disrespect. We want every moment we have with them to be fulfilling. Most of us

> What most of us desire from our horses is performance without intimidation, obedience without dominance, fun without disrespect.

spend time with horses for pleasure, usually at considerable financial and personal cost, and what we want most is to enjoy them, but that doesn't mean it will always be easy.

THE EQUINE RULEBOOK

To achieve a learning curve, you have to leave the comfort of the plateau. The need to keep climbing and progressing is what has always driven me. I used to be very competitive – and I still am – but I've learnt to channel this competitive drive in a more positive direction. To my mind, training a horse isn't about you winning and him losing: within a horse's social group everyone always plays fair, so it's far too easy for us to fix it so that he loses against us. Humans don't play fair for a number of reasons, but often it's because we don't really know the rules, rather than because we wish to be deliberately cruel, or it's because we have run out of options and are acting out of frustration.

> Understand why you're doing what you're doing and you'll be well on the way to analysing and solving your own problems and, eventually, preventing the majority of them

> True success is about setting up a 'win-win' situation for you and your horse.

This book is intended to be your guide to playing by equine rules. The aim is to provoke some thought, encourage you to reconsider whether your methods are as effective as they might be, and to provide some suggestions and alternatives. True success is about setting up a 'win-win' situation for you and your horse. As the controlling influence and the supposedly superior mind, it's up to you to learn the skills you need.

YOU CAN NEVER KNOW TOO MUCH

I'm lucky enough to have made a living out of horsemanship while also on my learning curve, but, more than that, what has inspired me to keep learning are the challenges which my own horses have thrown at me over the years. Even now, when I deal with many hundreds of horses in the course of a year, my idea of pleasure, stimulation and relaxation is to play with my own animals and try to reach the next stage of enlightenment. Because that's what it is. This book and my recent demonstrations represent where I am now on the learning curve. In a few

years time, with the benefit of the new learning experiences I hope are to come, I may modify my methods yet again as I inch further along the road travelled by so many horsemen before me. In the meantime, I try to learn from every horse and person I come across on the way.

Nothing I do is so precious that I'd never change it. You can only evolve in your thinking and be open to learning and progress in your horsemanship if you have this attitude. Everyone you come across will have something to offer, even if it's only to confirm to you how you don't want to do things. This is where the horses with severe behavioural problems I've dealt with over the years have been so influential. Dealing with horses that are difficult or even dangerous to ride has forced me to seek solutions and methods of communication other than riding, stripping down the process to its simplest, barest and most obvious forms to try to win back trust and co-operation. And often, being faced with such a huge challenge yet having nothing to lose has forced me to think beyond my normal boundaries and act beyond my comfort zone. It's these horses that have given me the biggest rush when what I've tried works. It's also these troubled equines that have taught me to see failure as part of learning and the opportunity to try something new. They've also taught me to know when to give up.

PRESSURE PRINCIPLE

For me, getting a precarious toe-hold back on the ladder of communication, from where I can slowly start inching my way up, means working the horse from the ground, teaching him the basic principle of moving away from

pressure, in whatever form it takes, in order to find release. When that moment comes, however small it is or however long it takes, I can reward the horse for good behaviour.

But this is a not just a system for problem horses – as you will see for yourself as you follow this guide – it benefits every horse of any age, ability or stage of training and gives them a good foundation from which to progress.

Monty Roberts, Pat Parelli, Ray Hunt, Rob Hoekstra, Jennie Loriston-Clarke and Andy Andrews have all challenged and inspired my thinking, and I am very grateful to them. However, you can't just throw loads of ingredients into a pie and expect it to come out perfect. If you do and it works, then it's luck rather than judgement, and you won't know how to repeat it! So what I've done with the knowledge I've got so far is develop a logical system, which, like a good recipe, can be shared with others and repeated with good results in all kinds of circumstances, even by those with limited time, facilities or experience. The proof of the pudding is in the eating, as they say, and countless horses have proved to me that this system is a good one, but I sincerely hope that more time and further experience will refine it even more in the years to come.

The basis of my work is this: I'm convinced that the majority of evasions in horses (from a slight lack of co-operation to a full-blown behavioural problem – all varying degrees of evasion) are the result of failing to cope with the three types of pressure – physiological, psychological and emotional – inflicted on them in the course of their domestic lives. These evasions manifest themselves as a slow response, no response or hyper response to whatever you ask.

YOU CAN DO IT

When it comes to furthering their horse's education or solving problems, many owners either settle for a compromise or enlist the help of an 'expert', perhaps because they think that they don't have the time, knowledge, experience or ability to teach their horses themselves. *But they do.* The methods outlined in this guide can take as little as 20 minutes a day, and don't require any special facilities or equipment, other than a halter, a 4m (12ft) rope and a long line. All it takes is common sense, a basic understanding of the horse's psyche and a willingness to stick to a logical system that will clarify and expand the lines of communication between horse and handler.

LOVE OR NOT?

One of the first things to realize is that horses do not give love as we humans give it, and they don't understand our insistence that they should love us just because we love them. Horses understand respect and pecking order. Until you can communicate to the horse that you are in charge, the horse will not respect you. Establishing this respect does not require the use of force, whips or spurs. It requires that the horse learns to trust you enough to yield physically, psychologically and emotionally to your requests and decisions.

How to use this book

The system described in this book tackles the issues of physiological, psychological and emotional pressure in three easy stages, and it will help you to develop a horse that is mentally and physically balanced and comfortable, one with whom you can safely have fun and explore whatever possibilities interest you.

PART ONE IS ABOUT GROUNDWORK

For me, the communication process starts by working the horse from the ground, teaching him the basic principle of moving away from pressure, in whatever form it takes, in order to find release. The simplest way to introduce the horse to the idea of pressure and release is to start with a rope halter. I put pressure on the horse's nose and poll, and I release it the moment he stops resisting and steps in the direction I'm asking. The horse is doubly rewarded for his co-operation: firstly by instant release of the pressure and secondly with praise from the handler. It doesn't take horses very long to realize what they have to do to make life easy for themselves, and that responding to my simple request is a fast route back to the comfort zone!

PART TWO IS ABOUT DISTANCE TRAINING

It's all very well moving your horse around when you're standing next to him, but does he still listen when you're at a distance? The next step is to develop the system further by sending him right away from you with a flick of the rope at his quarters until he is circling around you. He should stop him at the lightest pressure on the halter, or, better still, the first indication from you that you are about to take up pressure on the line. Eventually, the horse should become so attuned to your body language that he could be directed with just your finger tips. This is the beginning of teaching him self-balance – once he's learnt not to lean – and he will carry this concept through to his ridden work.

PART THREE IS ABOUT RIDDEN COMMUNICATION

Ridden problems are invariably reflected in groundwork. If the horse is heavy, lazy and unresponsive in hand, he'll be the same under saddle. The principles of teaching a horse lightness and self-carriage are much simpler than you might think, and the answers are in your groundwork. By asking him to carry himself during your rope circling and long reining sessions, you prepare the horse physically. Laying solid and permanent foundations in this way will make it easy for the horse to stay light, engaged, balanced and forward, even with the additional weight of a rider. The result? A 'virtuous circle' – the horse feels physically comfortable and capable of doing as he is asked, and has learnt to respond immediately to subtle pressure, so the rider can give minimal aids and enjoy the ride without interfering.

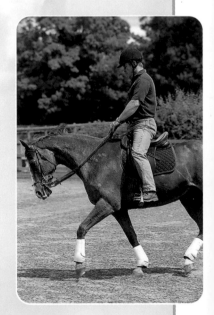

Finally, after these three practical chapters, there is one further section. This deals with so-called problem horses and offers some suggestions on how to find out what is wrong and then put it right. It also looks at some of the more common difficulties people experience with their horses and provides solutions anyone can try.

Try it yourself

This system does work, but I don't expect you to just take my word for it. Plenty of people out there are only too ready to give unproven advice, so I would expect you to want to see real results.

With any form of learning or new technique, look carefully at the whole process to see if it makes sense and works for your horse. Understand why you're doing what you're doing and you'll be well on the way to analyzing and solving your own problems and, eventually, preventing the majority of them.

Some owners are so used to the existing state of lack of respect and non co-operation between themselves and their animals, they might not even think they have a problem. Only in extreme cases are 'problem' horses raging, rearing, life-threatening monsters; more often, the signs of confusion, lack of understanding and disrespect manifest themselves in much more subtle ways. How many people do you know who have horses that won't load, stand still, tie up, hack out, be clipped, caught, wormed, tacked up, rugged up, groomed, lunged … with complete ease and total co-operation, at all times and in all places?

Some people's expectations of their horse are so low, they just feel grateful that they can ride him or her in some form or fashion. But wherever there's a problem, there's a good reason why the horse started behaving that way in the first place. It's time to ask ourselves when, how and why these vital clues in the horse's behaviour and attitude are ignored or mishandled, and examine the methods that keep producing the same problems.

PUTTING IT INTO PRACTICE

Over the years I've come to realize that my techniques are best taught to the rider as well as the horse. This way both understand what is expected of them and there is less room for confusion.

Do you need to read this book?

Ask yourself:
▷ Am I completely satisfied with my relationship with my horse?
▷ Do I regularly challenge and reassess my own thinking and motivation as a rider and handler?
▷ Is my horse a pleasure to ride, handle and own in every respect?
▷ Does she trust me in all things at all times?
▷ Will she transfer this trust to others and behave impeccably with them too?
▷ Do I accept responsibility for the way my horse behaves and am I able to change any negative aspects of that behaviour?
▷ Is my horse physically as strong and balanced as she can possibly be in order to enjoy her work and carry it out with ease?
▷ Do I believe I currently enjoy the highest and most subtle level of communication and understanding I can have with my horse?

If the answer to any of the above is even a tentative no, then read on. As I've already said, everyone has something to offer, even if it's only to confirm how you don't want to do things.

I used to want to help horses, until I realized how one-dimensional that was. I couldn't help all of the horses all of the time, and I wasn't doing them any favours when I returned them to owners who didn't understand the system I'd been using. So I decided to help people help their horses instead. That's when I stopped using the round pen, which has become such a familiar sight to those involved in 'natural' horsemanship. I stopped using it because most people don't have one. The only thing I use now is the horse's intelligence and the handler's understanding.

Thus, this book isn't just about training horses. It's about training you to train your horse. As a horse lover, I hope you'll do just that.

Ten rules of effective training

Read and digest the following before you get started on your horse!

1 Devote yourself to educating your horse logically. Every horse is born with the mind of a wild animal, and his fears are only overcome with repeated exposure to new experiences. His resulting behaviour is determined by how pleasant the experience proves to be. So if your horse is resistant to something, it's probably because a negative experience has 'taught' him to dislike it.

2 Don't set your horse up for failure. When things are going well it can be tempting to try to keep them going as long as possible, but good horsemanship is about knowing when to stop.

3 Be honest about your horse's abilities. Consider his physical, mental and emotional capacities – the limitations of his personality as well as his strengths.

4 Be versatile. If what you're doing isn't making any difference, improve or change your training methods. The skills you need to do this are the ability to watch, listen, ask and learn as much as you can, all your life.

5 Break down what you have to do into logical, manageable chunks that fit in with your time and lifestyle, so you can check progress and always know what you are working on and towards. Forcing a procedure through to the bitter end is not necessarily the most effective way to train a horse. What's important is that you regularly make some kind of progress, no matter how small, and that it is you who takes the decision to stop at a good moment, not the horse who stops at a bad one.

6 Ensure that you are being clear, fair, persistent and consistent in all your requests. There must be no grey areas, no bribery, no empty threats and no nagging if the horse is already trying his best. This also goes for any others who handle your horse. Teach them how to react when you're not there and explain why, so your horse gets a completely consistent reaction to his behaviour every time.

7 Pay attention to detail – the little things really do matter. If your horse barges past you to the field or won't stand still to be mounted, you'll find it hard to command instant respect and obedience in other things.

8 Make sure your domestic management is conducive to the horse co-operating. A horse that has freedom to move, graze and socialize with other horses for several hours a day is far less likely to develop abnormal behaviour and other hang ups.

9 Strength is not the answer. Even the smallest foal will get his own way if it comes to a battle of strength, and long-term it's the battle of wills that needs to be won. You'll do this by rewarding good behaviour, thus leaving a positive lasting impression, rather than punishing bad behaviour, which will cause resentment.

10 Take the time to build firm foundations to allow the horse to understand each stage and the rider to develop co-ordination and understanding, and logical progress will follow.

Just so you know where I'm coming from...

My mother was keen on horses, so as a child I spent many weekends around them. This is where my love affair started, although I didn't learn to ride properly until I was 11 years old, when I went to York Riding School, which was run by a Major Cole.

Major Cole was a huge influence in my life. To me he was old and looked very frail, but that didn't make him any less scary! He never held back when he was shouting at you, but he was always constructive. I laugh now when I look back at it. He used to shout at us kids as though we were in training for National Service, and it had exactly the same effect as similar treatment did on young recruits later on in my army days: it made us want to do well, to earn the praise that lay underneath all that bluster.

Major Cole was actually a very kind man, and a lot of his phrases stuck with me to the extent that I now find myself using them when I'm doing demonstrations! 'What are you trying to be – a one-man band?' and 'Everything that could possibly flap is flapping!' are just two examples.

One day – for reasons I've long forgotten – Major Cole got on one of the school ponies, an idle chap called Taffy. To put it kindly, we'd always thought Taffy was a bit of a mule: he wouldn't go forward and went about with his nose poked out. But, with the Major on board, before my very eyes this 'mule' turned into the most amazing, forward-going, self-carried

light pony I had ever seen in my life. Yet none of us could see the Major doing anything; it was like magic, and it stuck in my mind forever. I guess that was my first lesson in the 'less is more' school of thought that I now try to live by.

Once I had proven my worth, Major Cole used to let me ride all his new ponies, whether they were difficult or not. One day he said to me, 'Young Richard how many times have you fallen off?' 'I don't fall off,' I replied cockily. He eyed me with a knowing look and the

next time I went to ride he had a little pony called Dianna tacked up for me. Within five minutes I was eating the riding school floor. At the time I didn't understand why he had done that, but as time went on I realized that around horses you never get cocky or think you are too good, they are such good levellers and will quickly remind you who you are.

FLICKA SHOWS ME HOW IT'S DONE

As soon as I had had a couple of lessons I knew I just had to have my own pony. My mother didn't have much money and worked very hard for what she did have, so she said to me that for every pound I saved, she would equal it.

For the next two years I mowed lawns, washed cars and opted for money in my savings account instead of presents at birthdays and Christmas. Finally, with Mum's contribution, I had enough money to buy Flicka, a 13.2hh palomino pony: he cost £375 with rugs and tack. He was stabled about seven miles away, and every weekday after school I would cycle there and back.

For the next six months Flicka put me on the floor on a daily basis. I knew this pony could do it all, but he certainly made me work for it. To this day, I am sure Flicka was trying to teach me an invaluable lesson – that I didn't have an automatic right to a fantastic pony; I had to earn it. It took six months but when it came it was worth it. With Flicka I showjumped, hunted and did the whole pony club thing. We kept Flicka until he died; I was married and in the army by then, but my mother felt that as he had been such

> I am sure Flicka was trying to teach me an invaluable lesson – that I didn't have an automatic right to a fantastic pony; I had to earn it. It took six months but when it came it was worth it.

a part of the family she just couldn't bear to sell him on.

We were a formidable team, and when I look back, I realize just how much Flicka taught me. I'll explain more later on.

WET BEHIND THE EARS

At 18 years old I knew that I had to leave home and broaden my horizons, so I decided to join the army. I really wanted to join the King's Troop Royal Horse Artillery, as I had spent a week with them when I was 17 on a prospective recruit-type programme. However, when it came to me joining, my recruiting office, obviously desperate to make up numbers for the local Yorkshire regiment, the 4th/7th Royal Dragoon Guards, told me that I had to join them. Being a bit wet behind he ears, I agreed, and off I went to learn how to be a tankie.

Don't get me wrong, I had a great time; I loved the camaraderie of being in the army, and to this day I miss the laughs and the really basic humour, but at the time I also desperately missed the horses. I managed to get a transfer to the Rhine Army Polo Association as a groom, then a year or so later I went back to my own regimental stables, which happened to be situated next door to the Blues and Royals Saddle Club, which was run by Keith Burns, a Life Guard (in the 'Trooping of the Colour', Life Guards wear red tunics and have white plumes and the Blues and Royals have blue tunics and red plumes). Keith persuaded me to apply for a transfer to the Life Guards. He said to me, 'Try and be the best, learn to clean the ceremonial kit and do well in your first year doing duties at Whitehall, and then I will make sure that you get on the Military Equitation Long Course.' In 1986, a few days before Prince Andrew married Sarah Ferguson, I arrived at Knightsbridge Barracks to start my time as a cavalryman.

I have to admit that I did do well in riding school, where all new recruits learn how to ride, look after their horses and clean the 'kit' (the

> The most important thing I learnt on that course was how to break things down into easily learnable chunks … I think it has been of great benefit to me in my work with horses and people.

term for your everyday uniform and ceremonial kit). There were two reasons I did well. One was that I had the advantage of being able to ride, and the other was that although I was a lot older than most of the recruits, I wanted to do it so badly. At last I was in a job where I could actually work with horses, and be involved in the training of both

horses and soldiers.

In 1987 I went on the Military Equitation Long Course, which was in Melton Mowbray and lasted for six months. It was the most amazing experience and it taught me many things about myself. On the course, all students were given a fully trained horse, a half-trained horse and an un-backed horse – the idea being to bring each horse up to the next level over the six months. At the end, we had to do a one-day event on our half-trained horses, which by then would, in theory, be fully trained!

I was a very shy person and not

very good at small talk – in fact I'm still like this – so, to prove my worth, I threw every ounce of myself into my horsemanship and riding. I was desperate for my superiors to see my commitment and enthusiasm, and to prove I was a valuable member of the team. However, the one thing that was noted (and I learnt about myself, too) was that I didn't like the constrictions of training horses in the military way. There are many aspects of it that I think have value, and I still use, but at the time, just occasionally, I felt my horse would have benefited from a different

approach: my report at the end of the course said that sometimes I found all the red tape difficult!

Of all the things I learnt on that course, the most important was how to break things down into easily learnable chunks, and how to communicate information to other people. This was vital – the purpose of the course was to teach me to be an instructor in the Knightsbridge Barracks, where 95 per cent of the recruits have never seen a horse and there are only 20 weeks to teach them to be able to walk, trot and canter, independently and as a quadrille! They also have to jump down a line of three-foot fences with no stirrups or reins, at the same time taking off their jackets and shouting their name, rank and number. Under these circumstances, to over-complicate the art of riding would have been disastrous, but once you've learnt how to make things simple, you can use this skill in many areas. I think it has been of great benefit to me in my work with horses and people.

Once I was back at Knightsbridge, it wasn't too long before I got my place on the Riding Staff, the team of instructors responsible for the backing of all the horses, known as Cavalry Blacks, that came over from Ireland, and the training of all new recruits. It was a time of great laughter. We were all boys together – with the whole bravado thing – not wanting to show that it was pretty scary getting on these horses for the first time; a bit like taking our lives into our own hands. There were bodies everywhere, and the harder we were thrown off, the harder we all laughed.

MONTY ROBERTS AND JOIN-UP

One day we were all instructed to attend a demonstration being given to the Queen by some American chap who 'reckoned he could back a horse in 30 minutes'. Well you can imagine a group of soldiers' sceptical view of that.

But the American was Monty Roberts, and he did back a horse in 30 minutes. Were we impressed?… Of course not, he had obviously done it before and there was aniseed in his pocket. That's how he got those horses following him, we had him sussed, or so we thought. Our boss, however, was very impressed, and ended up going out to California and learning the technique from Monty. He came back to barracks and said, 'Right lads this is how we are doing it from now on.' Myself and another bloke were assigned to help.

That is where I learnt about 'join-up' and the whole starting process. To be honest, there couldn't have been a better platform for Monty, because if it worked with these wild and woolly creatures that were sent over from Ireland, join-up would work with anything. I was amazed by the results. Nobody got dumped at all that year! But what amazed me most was that it wasn't just the backing process that improved but everything from handling to loading, and so on.

A few months after the first demonstration, Monty was doing another one at a nearby stud, and our boss said he was going: did anyone want to join him? I was the only person to volunteer. When we arrived, Monty had no rider to use for the demo. At that point, I had never done the join-up process itself, but my services were volunteered, and from that day on I became Monty's UK-based rider. I used all my leave to do the demonstrations, and just listened and learnt.

The following winter I arrived at the venue for a demo a day early. All the horses for the week had arrived and the pen was up in the school, so I thought I'd be helpful and make a start. I was working away with a youngster when I saw Monty walking towards me. He was slightly amazed, since he hadn't actually shown me how to do anything.

'You and I need to talk,' he said, and I was really worried! But he was full of praise and said that maybe we should think about doing something together, as I was based in Britain. That was when I applied for voluntary redundancy from the army.

GOING TO CALIFORNIA

Once the redundancy came through, Sam (my wife) and I moved to California for a couple of months. It was a fantastic experience. I worked mainly with the racehorses and did a lot with starting stall problems.

Occasionally local yards would call Monty for help with problem horses. One day a call came through from a yard that backed young horses. They had a youngster that bucked like stink as soon as its feet touched the dirt, throwing the rider. To date, nobody had managed to stay on. Monty told them to bring it on over, which they did, along with their own rider.

Now try to visualize the situation. Monty doing join-up with the horse, while the yard owner and his rider and a few others were on the other side of the pen. To me, the rider looked like a real cowboy; he had a

blue shirt, a bandana around his neck, a black leather waistcoat, wrangler jeans and a belt with the biggest buckle on, and, of course, the obligatory cowboy boots and hat. He walked with that John Wayne swagger and chewed tobacco. I was seriously impressed – I think secretly I've always fancied being a cowboy – I couldn't wait to see him ride.

Monty had the horse tacked up and started long lining. At the appropriate moment, he signalled to the rider to come down and ride. The cowboy swaggered down the steps, went to the big wooden doors, and reappeared a few minutes later, obviously completely terrified, apparently half his previous size, with a back protector done up very tightly and a crash hat pulled firmly on his head. All signs of the swagger had gone. It was at this point that I saw clearly how easy it is to be cocky and criticize when you're safely watching. It's very different when you have to 'walk the talk'.

As Monty said afterwards, he took one look at the rider and knew that the horse wasn't the problem. Because the rider was so terrified, he gave the horse no confidence, and because he wasn't able to balance himself, it didn't take much for him to fall off, so, in effect, the yard had trained the horse to get rid of his rider. I truly believe that until that day, the horse didn't understand that the rider was supposed to stay on. Monty asked me to jump on, the horse was absolutely fine, and within a few days we had him going round the track like an old pro.

While I was with Monty, I did a few trips up to Santa Anita racetrack in Los Angeles, where I learnt a thing or two about equine egos, too. I was

given permission to ride on the track while dealing with a stalls problem.

My job was to ride a mare out of the stalls. She didn't refuse to go into the stalls, she just refused to come out! We would get her to stand in the stalls and then get another horse to gallop past while I encouraged her to leave the stalls and give chase. The lead horse would then be pulled up steadily, allowing the problem mare to catch up and pass. Her confidence in her own ability and enthusiasm for racing built up and it worked a treat.

On our return to the UK, it was decided that Newmarket would be a

good area to move to as Monty was very much into the racing industry and there were a lot of problems with horses refusing to go into starting stalls. No matter how well bred or fast they are, they can't race if they don't start.

Although we stuck it out for a year and we did some good work with the horses, it became clear I was never going to be accepted into the world of racing. I found it something of a closed shop and I hadn't done my apprenticeship, so to speak. Things weren't looking too good – I had had to sub-let my yard through the winter and felt like giving up – when a couple called Tom and Pauline James sent us a pony that was to change our lives. We worked hard with this pony and once he went home, Tom and Pauline were so delighted with the result that they called *Your Horse* magazine and told the editorial team all about me. The magazine dispatched a journalist by the name of Jo Sharples. She could see that there was serious mileage in what I was trying to do – enough mileage to provide features of interest to the readers for the next four years, as it turned out! I went on to produce two books: *Understanding Your Horse* with *Your Horse* editor Lesley Bayley and *From Birth to Backing* with Jo. Then I decided that I needed some time to think things through and come up with something new.

UNLOCK YOUR HORSE'S TALENT

It took nearly two years, but what I came up with was what you'll find in this book. Basically, I decided I needed to take all that I had learnt from problem horses and put it to use in every day riding situations and for normal schooling problems. This book condenses that knowledge into a simple, user-friendly system. What I also realized was that it isn't the horse I should be re-schooling, but the owner, so that he or she can take the pleasure and responsibility of training their own horse. Meanwhile, the horse is kept in the environment he is used to and the owner gains the knowledge and confidence to deal with him there. I could see that it was no good just me being able to ride all these difficult horses. Ultimately, I had to hand them back into the situation that had created the problems, and might cause them again.

THE FUTURE

My passion is my own horses, and in an ideal world I'd spend far more time at home with them and Sam and our three gorgeous sons. I love eventing and showjumping, but because I spend a lot of hours on the road and am not home to put in the work, it would be unfair of me to pull my horses out of the field and expect great things. Yet, I know they hold the secret of my way forward, and I'm itching to spend time finding out what they still have to teach me.

1 Basic groundwork

The nature of the horse

Watching today's competition horse soar effortlessly over solid timber fences, dance obediently within the confines of a dressage arena or carefully assess a course of coloured showjumps, it's easy to forget that he is behaving in a way entirely contrary to his nature.

> In domesticating the horse and training him for our purposes, we take advantage of many characteristics that are intrinsic to his nature – his sociability, curiosity, understanding of hierarchy, his natural strength, athleticism and turn of speed.

What has happened to the timid creature of flight who roamed the plains with his herd for thousands of years, whose every instinct tells him to flee from confined spaces and fear weight on his back? Nothing has happened: he's still there. Buried at the heart of every domestic horse are the instincts bred into him by his wild ancestors; it's just that some are buried more deeply than others, depending on the handling and amount of conditioning he has received.

In domesticating the horse and training him for our purposes, we take advantage of many characteristics that are intrinsic to his nature – his sociability, curiosity, understanding of hierarchy, his natural strength, athleticism and turn of speed. There's nothing wrong with doing this, as long as we don't confuse the horse's willing nature with his inherent nature. No matter how hard we try to overcome it, we must respect the fact

that he is a flight animal at heart. Failure to recognize this can cause immense psychological damage to the horse and lies at the root of many training problems.

Fortunately, the recent trend in horsemanship has been to take greater account of the horse's natural inclinations during the course of training. As well as being more humane than some 'traditional' methods, so-called 'natural' horsemanship (training that is sympathetic to and in accordance with the horse's natural instincts) is also highly effective – assuming that your goal is to have a horse that is content, obedient and comfortable physically, mentally and emotionally.

However, while I support the principles of natural horsemanship that can lead to these results, I've also seen the system misused by owners or abused by trainers jumping on the bandwagon. Horse owners

Horse owners are naturally susceptible to the idea that they could be doing things better or more sympathetically with their horses, but sympathy is very different to sentiment.

THE HORSE IS A FLIGHT ANIMAL

No matter how hard we try to overcome his desire to run, we must respect the fact that the horse is a flight animal at heart. Failure to recognize this can cause immense psychological damage to the horse and lies at the root of many training problems. This sequence shows how the horse is designed to stop, turn and run, even from a flat-out gallop. The instincts governing this desire to flee will over-ride all but the most dedicated training, such as that undergone by police horses.

are naturally susceptible to the idea that they could be doing things better or more sympathetically with their horses, but sympathy is very different to sentiment. Some owners who shelter beneath the natural horsemanship banner have misinterpreted (or been misled about) its true principles and, as a result, become less, rather than more, effective with their horses. Of course, we all want to have a special bond with our horses, and it's tempting to think he will 'love' us more for making sure he has a 'nice time' when he's with us. But this can result in us being pushed around by him, especially if we feel a bit guilty about the time we spend with him due to work, family and social pressures. A horse does not love you more because you give him more treats. His attachment to anyone is dependent on respect, and he'll be most respectful towards those who make it clear where the boundaries lie. As in a herd situation, he'll only feel safe and secure when he has a leader (owner) he can respect and trust to make good decisions on his behalf. After all, in the wild, his life depends on it.

Communication

Before I go any further, it's important to explain that my training philosophy is based around pressure and release (or question and answer).

PRESSURE AND RELEASE

Why do I place so much importance on pressure and release? Because it's what makes most sense to the horse – it's the language horses use to communicate with and discipline each other within their own herd environment. It is the essence of all interaction between horses, an equine tool that is useful in our own dealings with them. I emphasize, however, that by 'pressure', I do *not* mean pain.

Pressure comes in three forms – visual, tactile and emotional – and usually follows that order of progression.

1 **Visual Pressure** is face-pulling, ears back, walking boldly into another horse's space to move them around. It is the first course of non-contact action.

2 **Tactile Pressure** is biting and kicking. It is used to back up visual pressure.

3 **Emotional Pressure** is ignoring the horse, sending it away from the group for unacceptable behaviour. It can be used in isolation or as a final resort after visual and tactile pressure, and is often the tactic employed by older horses to put cheeky youngsters in their place.

VISUAL PRESSURE

A mare uses visual pressure when she has a foal at foot, but this is not to prove her dominance, rather it is to keep him respectful and so safe. There is no stronger bond than that of a mare and her offspring, yet she doesn't use kisses and cuddles to make her foal respectful, nor does she have equipment such as head collars and ropes. What she does have is the ability to move her foal around, and in the language of the horse, this indicates she must be obeyed! A horse that controls movement and direction is the one in charge, and this is the way she achieves the respect of other horses. In the case of the mare and foal, it is

INCREASING PRESSURE

Within a group, horses will always start with visual pressure, especially in a wild herd situation where tactile pressure might result in an injury and a lame horse is the predator's next meal. Here you can see that Molly (the black older mare on the right) doesn't like the fact that Scarlet (the young chestnut on the left) is getting too close, so she pulls a face.

Scarlet chooses not to heed the message (right), although it's pretty clear even to the most unobservant human what Molly is trying to say! This forces Molly to back up her visual threat with action – a nip on the neck.

This has the desired effect (below). Scarlet becomes very attentive and reacts immediately to subsequent visual pressure from Molly. You'll notice that this highly effective disciplining was carried out without any noise, violence or actual pain, in a way which obviously made absolute sense to Scarlet without damaging her physically, mentally or emotionally. As trainers, we have a lot to learn from the way horses interact with each other.

> A horse that controls movement and direction is the one in charge, and this is the way she achieves the respect of other horses.

not only a matter of discipline but also of safety that the foal responds to his mother's pressure, does as he is told and stays where he is put. As you've probably seen, youngsters of any species are easily distracted and can wander off. It's very important to the foal's survival that the mother is able to gain his focus and attention and, simple though it sounds, she does this by getting him to look her in the eye.

When a horse gives you 'one eye', he is only giving you his passing attention; when he gives you both eyes, he gives you his focus and, ultimately, his respect. The horse's eyes are on the side of his head to allow for maximum peripheral vision, so the foal will pretty much always have his mother in sight. However, this does not mean she has his full focus. To get this, she will need the foal to turn around to face her. Her first option won't be to run up and grab him by the mane, neck or head, as we humans might be tempted to do. Instead, she will apply visual pressure, using her body language to push his quarters away and make him bring his head towards her. She then has his full attention and can move or position him wherever she wishes.

FOCUS ON YOU

Understanding that being in charge is about taking control of movement and direction is vital to us as horse handlers and trainers. How many times have you walked around your horse in the field or stable instead of asking him to move over, stepped back as he pushes towards the doorway at feed time or walked towards him, reeling in your lunge lines after a groundwork session? All these actions are telling your horse that he is in charge because he is in control of your movement – and horses are very good at training us to run around after them in this way! We thus confirm that our horse is above us in the pecking order, and issues of respect, or lack of it, invariably result.

Beware of even apparently minor issues of lack of respect, which many people appear happy to put up with or hardly notice. Attention to detail is important and can seriously affect your relationship with your horse. In a bright, talented or naturally dominant animal, which would otherwise be a pleasure to own, such details can represent the thin edge of a wedge since major difficulties are generally just the minor ones which have been mishandled, allowed to escalate and snowball out of control into a full-blown behavioural problem (see also 'My horse is stressed in the stable', p.147).

A horse that is high up the pecking order will not say, 'Excuse me,' and walk around another horse to get past. It will walk purposefully towards the horse's neck using visual pressure, and the other horse will automatically move out of the way in order to avoid the consequences, that is tactile pressure. You can do this too, by using your own positive body language – be assertive in your posture with shoulders squared (see above) to the horse and maintain a generally confident manner. If you are not like this by nature, then you need to recognize it and develop the skills you need to communicate better with your horse, just as you might take riding lessons to improve your technique in the saddle.

I don't want to get too hooked on the body language aspect of human to horse relationship as it has been covered many times before. I have also seen people get too over-sensitive about it, and try to change the way they are around a horse they have known for a long time. 'Don't fix what ain't broke' is a valuable adage. As long as you are being effective and getting the results you want from your horse, you are probably communicating on a subtle level with him without realizing it. However, body language is particularly important with nervous, traumatized or abused horses that have become wary and hypersensitive to all forms of pressure and are incapable of responding calmly to anything but the most subtle visual pressure.

TACTILE PRESSURE

Tactile pressure is not about beating your horse – a prod from your finger or a gentle nudge with your elbow is usually sufficient to get a response.

EMOTIONAL PRESSURE

Finally, emotional pressure is used when a horse is showing unacceptable behaviour and the herd leader drives them out of the herd until they have learnt their lesson. It was observing this form of discipline that led Monty Roberts to the join-up approach. (For more information on this, see Ground Training from a Distance, pp.54–81.)

Horses hate to be ignored or sent away from the group. Any attention, even apparently negative attention, is better than no attention in almost every case. For example, when you yell at a horse that is banging a door at feed time you will encourage him to continue doing it, as long as he gets a reaction from you – like a child showing off in front of friends. They know their behaviour is 'wrong' and they may get in trouble for it, but the enticement of your attention and focus drives them to do it anyway.

TACTILE PRESSURE

If it comes to the crunch and your horse is ignoring you, you must be prepared to do what another horse would do and apply effective tactile pressure. This is where many humans lose heart and get it wrong, and often choose to avoid the issue, not realizing the consequences as outlined in 'Focus on you', p.25. Given your size and weight against that of the horse, it can appear to be a losing battle, but remember this is not about strength or brutality. A prod from your finger will cause sufficient discomfort for the horse to move away, provided you have got some degree of mental focus through your body language first. Remember he can feel a fly landing on his skin –

if he chooses to ignore signals such as these then you really do need to concentrate on gaining his focus and respect through consistent firm handling and the halter work described on pp.44–45 to remind him of the rules of pressure.

Never raise your hand to your horse, or smack him with an open hand, as he should see your hand as some thing of comfort when you stroke him. It's the tool of reward, not punishment, and you should never cheat him by using it as the instrument of discipline. If he never knows what's coming, how can you expect him not to be confused? Remember, the success of your training lies in making your horse feel safe while he's in your presence.

THE 'INTO PRESSURE' ANIMAL

In certain situations, normally where the horse feels threatened, he will actually move into pressure, as opposed to away from it. Think about the last time a horse stood on your foot: when you went to push him off he probably leant into you, rather than moved away. You can also witness this in a much less painful way by watching how a horse can start to sway in response to a firm grooming, as he leans into every stroke of the brush against his body.

Horses move into pressure because it's a damage limitation response designed by Mother Nature. In the wild, dogs and other predators will always go for the vulnerable soft flesh under the belly, just in front of the stifle (where many horses are anxious and ticklish, probably for this very reason). If the horse pulls away, tearing the flesh in this area, the weight of the intestines increases the tear and results in certain death.

I experienced a gruesome example of this when I was working in Germany as a polo groom. We were walking the ponies back to the yard through a stream when one of them stepped on a stick that flipped up and made a small puncture wound in the soft flesh of her under belly. By the time we got the pony back to the yard, her intestines were falling out, even though the original hole had been tiny.

ATTENTION AND RESPECT

Like a senior herd member, I want my horse's focus, attention and respect when I'm working with him. Even though this horse is loose, you can see I've got his attention and he's making an effort to 'read' me. Don't underestimate the subtlety your horse is capable of. If you learn to operate on a level that is this subtle, physical force won't be necessary.

BE A PASSIVE LEADER

Horse people who think that by not being assertive with their horse, they are being kind should be aware that the way horses choose to live in their herd environment shows that they need and appreciate a leader. It is what they understand, what is natural to them and what makes them feel physically, mentally and emotionally secure.

In a herd situation there are two types of leader – the alpha leader who rules by dominance, and the passive leader who leads by example. The passive leaders are usually chosen by other members of the herd and are followed willingly, while alphas use force to declare their place in the herd.

Passive leaders are quiet and consistent in their day-to-day behaviour and appear not to need to continually declare their position in the herd. Alphas, on the other hand, are often very pushy, sometimes going as far as using unprovoked attacks on subordinates for the simple reason of declaring their dominance. As a result of this behaviour, the majority of the horses in the herd will actually avoid all contact with the alpha because horses are designed to save energy in their day-to-day activities, in case they really need to run for their lives. By following a passive leader who uses the least amount of energy (and who isn't constantly forcing other horses to use theirs), the horses help to ensure their own survival.

Passive leaders have earned their position in the herd by showing the other horses that they can be dependable in their passive behaviour from one day to the next, and this is the type of behaviour that you should try to base your training on. You are aiming for your horse to view you as his passive leader.

So how does this affect your training and handling of your horse? Well the simple fact that equines are not confrontational by nature and definitely prefer a quiet and easy life if given a choice, means that they are ready to be told what to do, and actually feel more comfortable when they know someone else, rather than themselves, is in charge.

As I said above, the safety and security of the herd is down to the leader, therefore, he knows you would not ask him to do something that might cause him harm. This is why, unlike some other trainers, I talk about aiming for a 49:51 per cent partnership with a horse, with the rider/handler having the controlling share. In the horse's language, a 50:50 partnership is very uncomfortable. Who should he turn to if he feels insecure? Who's making the decisions, and can they be trusted? In the absence of anyone else taking charge, he may well decide he ought to. This is not about being bossy or dominating your horse; this is about having the final say in a potentially dangerous situation. And to the horse, everything from wearing a saddle to

> Horses are not social climbers, once they know their place within the pecking order, they are quite happy to stay there as long as it gives them an easy life and they feel safe.

walking past a dustbin is a potentially dangerous situation unless he has confidence in you.

Uncertainty and insecurity can lead to relatively minor problems that spoil your enjoyment of your horse, such as him refusing to be clipped, loaded, turned out, tied up, hosed down or left alone. Indeed, such 'problems' are so common that they are considered acceptable behaviour in many yards. Yet they all start with a basic lack of respect and trust, and poor communication between horse and handler. If your horse can do the right thing (and knows what the 'right thing' is in each case – it may not be as obvious to him as it is to you) then generally he will do it as it is not in a horse's make-up to be belligerent. Horses become difficult because in effect, without realizing it, that is what we have trained them to do (see 'Going to California', p.18, for an example).

By taking the time to build trust, explain clearly what you want and reward correct behaviour even in everyday procedures, you'll reduce the potential for those damaging power struggles that might otherwise emerge and you'll also set a pattern of behaviour which will stand you in good stead for the challenges ahead. Horses are not social climbers, once they know their place within the pecking order, they are quite happy to stay there as long as it gives them an easy life and they feel safe. A horse will always choose the path of least resistance.

OVERCOMING WORRIES

You can do all sorts of exercises with your horse to gain his trust and get him to see you as the leader, so when he is faced with a worrying situation, such as going through water, he looks to you for reassurance. This exercise, which can be attempted after you've completed the work in this chapter, is one of many that you can try to teach your horse to trust your judgement as well as become less inclined to be spooky.

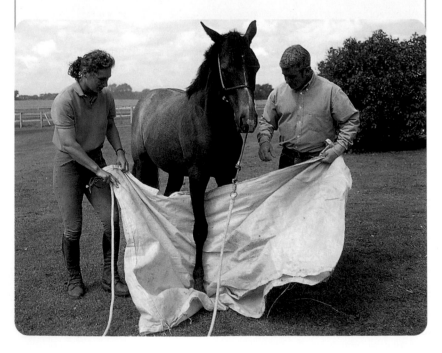

GAIN YOUR HORSE'S RESPECT

Horses do not respect aggression, and in fact have a deep instinct to flee from it, so getting respect is absolutely not a matter of 'showing him who's boss'. But they do like to reassure themselves by 'knowing who's boss', which is a very different thing. Like a child with a strict teacher, who knows he won't get away with handing in homework late or throwing notes in class and because of this learns better and is more pleasant to be around, so it should be with your horse: that's why you need his respect.

Fortunately, since it forms the basis of every relationship, not just the horse/human one, getting respect is not as hard as it sounds! What's more it doesn't take an expert or even an experienced rider to achieve it.

But how do you get it?

Despite 6,000 years of domestication, the horse's instincts are still largely developed for survival in the wild, this is true even for an animal bred for showing and kept almost constantly stabled. (In fact, many animal behaviourists believe the legendary 'cleverness' of native ponies is because they are most often kept in feral situations and are, therefore, making better daily use of their instincts.)

> **Horses respect firmness not aggression, empathy not sentiment, consistency not inflexibility, persistence not nagging.**

So, getting your horse's respect is a simple matter of understanding his natural instincts, learning how they govern his behaviour and making allowances for it. Horses respect

INSTANT RESPONSE

In most situations a horse will only have to use visual pressure to get the desired response from a horse that is lower in the pecking order. Here the grey immediately moves out of the way of the chestnut.

firmness not aggression, empathy not sentiment, consistency not inflexibility, persistence not nagging.

I say again: do not to confuse respect with liking. I have liked a great many of my teachers but that doesn't mean I respected all of them. I had an English teacher who was very modern in his approach to teaching and believed we should all 'express' ourselves … so we did, which meant we didn't do anything except fool around and be a nuisance; I didn't achieve anything productive in those lessons, and the teacher was unable to turn the class around because he'd started off being too relaxed and no one respected him. For all that he was a great and forward-thinking guy. The flip side to this was my maths teacher; he was a ferocious disciplinarian who stamped on the smallest misdemeanour and was intolerant of mistakes. Consequently, I feared him. Fear did to me what it does to horses and humans alike   it

made me shut down, so I was incapable of learning. It was like a form of paralysis. Again I had no respect for that teacher because he gave no guidance or encouragement.

The result of this education is that to this day I am very poor in both English and maths – I have a mental block. The subjects I did well in were those that had teachers whom I respected, who had a fair and consistent way of putting across their subject, who encouraged me when I was struggling and who praised when I succeeded. Remember, when you become your horse's teacher you need to be fair, consistent and quick with your praise.

I also believe that with respect will come trust especially during training. Respect and trust are your most powerful tools; they are better than any gadget you might buy. The best thing you can do for your horse is to have him safe, and emotionally and physically comfortable, when in your presence, whether handling or riding.

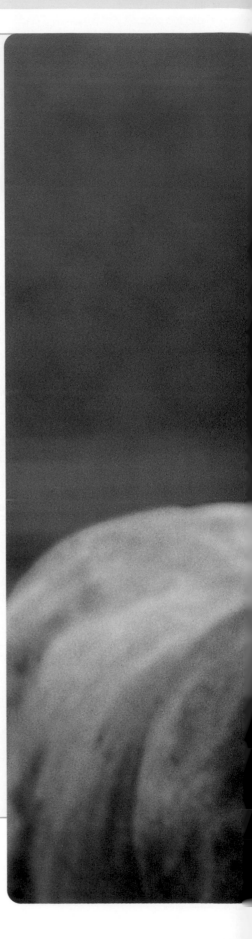

UNDERSTANDING THE FLIGHT INSTINCT

The majority of behavioural problems in horses arise as a result of their flight instinct being somehow mishandled, abused or misunderstood, so it should not be taken lightly. The horse is a flight animal, made to live in open spaces. His way of dealing with problems is to run, not fight, because this is where his best chance of survival lies. Nothing will totally eliminate the escape response, this relic of evolution from the equine psyche, although habituation of the type undergone by police horses in their training can alleviate it to a massive degree. This is why if a frightened horse is fighting restraint, it can have serious consequences: he truly believes he is fighting for his life. Likewise, being isolated and in a dark and confined space is not a situation a horse will normally put himself in. The fact that, with correct training, a horse will walk into a trailer or lorry is quite incredible. Even walking into a stable or being strapped into a rug represents the horse overcoming a major psychological barrier and is a sign of his enormous generosity and willingness to co-operate, and we must remember to give credit where it is due, rather than getting frustrated when he shows signs of reluctance. Yes, the horse must learn to do these things willingly in order to fit into domestic life and deal comfortably with the interaction he is to have with humans in the future. However, the humans who deal with him must also be sympathetic to the fact that thousands of years of evolution are telling the horse not to do what we are asking him to do, under any circumstances.

Something all horses are very sensitive to is fear. That's why negative reinforcement is not recommended as a training method, and why punishment for undesirable behaviour will simply panic and confuse them. When a horse is scared, all his attention is focused on escape, not on working out what he has done to deserve such treatment and learning his lesson for next time.

When horses do not behave as we wish, so long as no physical reason (such as pain) is involved, it is most often because we have not communicated well enough or we have unnatural expectations. Horses are perfect at being horses!

In the wild, the horse is game for predators, and he knows it. His flight instinct is a very effective way of avoiding them, but only if he listens carefully to the information his well-developed senses provide him with. Every horse handler, rider or trainer should understand the effect this has on the horse's reactions and learning. It is that instinctive reaction to run – without hanging around to analyze the situation and realize that the scary object is just the same dustbin they see every day for example – which causes the horse's illogical (to us) blind panic.

ACTING ON INSTINCT

Horses act on the information that their highly developed senses provide them with. Flared nostrils, wide eyes, high head carriage and cocked ears aim to maximize this horse's knowledge of his immediate environment and tell us a huge amount about his psychological state.

The senses

As mentioned earlier, I don't want to get too hooked on the body language aspect of the human to horse relationship. However, **observing your horse and understanding how he uses his body and senses will give you a lot of information about his mode of communication,** and essential feedback about his mood and understanding when you are working with him.

HEARING

Those radar ears are perfectly designed to pick out noises over a huge distance, as they would need to for horses to check what was happening on the 'bush telegraph'. As they can move independently of each other, they allow the horse to check up on more than one thing at once – one ear may be directed at something happening in the feed room, while the other is directed at another horse in the yard. You can use this ability to work out whether the horse is paying attention when schooling – generally, where his ears are, there is his focus also.

Horses can hear sounds higher and lower than we can and pick them up from a greater distance. Their wider range of hearing probably accounts for 'strange' or 'naughty' behaviour, such as shying at bicycles. It may not be the bicycle that has frightened him, but the high-pitched whistling of the wheels, beyond the range of human hearing.

A horse's hearing can be used as a schooling aid: they learn to respond to voice commands on the lunge or the 'click' of the tongue given for encouragement.

WHERE HIS EARS ARE, THERE IS HIS FOCUS

Pricked or forward ears (right) indicate the nature and location of the horse's interest at that moment. This is quite a friendly gesture and once the horse has satisfied his curiosity, the ears relax. Pinned or laid-back ears normally denote a form of aggressiveness, or perhaps anger. They are part of the repertoire of threatening gestures. When one horse approaches another with ears laid back (left), the message is along the lines of, 'Move or suffer the consequences.' When you are working with a horse and he pins back his ears, he's signalling his unhappiness with you or with something you are doing, or he's demonstrating aggressive behaviour. What exactly were you doing at the time? Tightening a girth? Approaching with a saddle? Timing will help you understand what your horse is trying to tell you.

EYES – THE MIRROR OF THE SOUL?

Said to be the mirror of the soul in humans, eyes certainly reflect mood in the horse! Soft, wide, dark eyes convey the impression of relaxation and mild curiosity. Eyes wide with fear or pain look very different, especially if they roll until the whites are showing. Normally, this action of the eye communicates fear and is accompanied by a raised head, alert ears, and a tense body. This body language signal tells us that the horse might be preparing to take flight to escape what he perceives to be a dangerous situation.

Tension around the eyes can also denote tension elsewhere – horses that are uncomfortably pressurized or generally unhappy often look concerned and as if they are 'frowning', or they may have 'worry wrinkles' around their eyes. A nervous horse will often show the whites of his eyes. While a 'soft' blinking eye is an outward sign that a horse is thinking and will often happen during schooling breaks, hence the old nagsman's phrase: 'If they're blinking, they're thinking.'

When you are riding in a group, pinned ears can be a classic warning that a horse feels threatened by another, so beware that he might follow his visual threat with a kick.

Most of the time the ears are flicking forward and back, especially when you are riding and the horse is dividing his attention between you and his surroundings. I always think that riding a horse whose ears are straining forward away from me gives a fair imitation of an equine V-sign from where the rider is sitting! Indeed most riders will have experienced the feeling of their mount being 'mentally absent' at such times.

Racehorses illustrate this point quite well. Normally, as they head down the homestretch, their ears will be flicking forward and back. Generally, if both ears are forward during the final strides in a race, the horse isn't concentrating on running as much as something that has appeared down the track ahead of him! Usually, others in the field will be in front of or far behind a horse racing with his ears forward, while horses that are 'neck and neck' in a duel for victory often have their ears pinned to their heads in challenge.

VISION

Horses have the largest eyes of any land mammal in proportion to their size, which goes some way to suggesting the importance of sight to them. They also have excellent night vision: it's thought that they see as well as dogs and owls in the dark.

Old nagsmen had a theory that if a horse had a small eye, or showed the white of an eye, it would be 'mean' or hard to train. There is, in fact, some physical basis for this reasoning. Because of eye placement in the skull and the huge size of the equine eye, the horse has almost 360-degree vision. A horse with a tiny, sunken eye loses a good deal of his peripheral vision and seems to spend lots of time worrying about what is happening around and behind him. Thus, it stands to reason that a small-eyed horse might be more cantankerous and difficult to train and handle.

Horses don't need to be able to differentiate colour precisely in the way which birds that survive on fruits and berries do, but they need a certain amount to help them see through the camouflage of a predator. An animal that can see some degree of colour is far harder to ambush.

The position of the eyes, set far back in the skull on the side of the head, is what enables horses to have almost all round vision, including nearly the entire area behind them, as well as the whole horizon. With his head level, a horse has just two narrow blind spots, one extending a few metres behind the rump and the other a few centimetres in front of the nose.

The length of the horse's nose, so cleverly designed to allow him to eat and watch at the same time, prevents him seeing the ground beneath his feet as he lifts his forehand to take off over a jump. So a horse cannot actually see what he is jumping and must rely on the image he had of the fence a couple of strides out.

PANORAMIC VISION

The horse's eyes are designed around his need to focus broadly on distant objects. The retina (the focusing screen at the back of the eye) has a 'sharp' horizontal strip, called the 'visual streak', across its lower part; this means that the horse sees clearly in a very wide but squat field. The horse will move his head and neck into various positions to fix on particular objects or views and cause the light rays to fall within this visual streak and clarify what he sees.

The downside of the horse's extraordinary panoramic vision is that his ability to bring close objects into sharp focus is more limited, particularly since he cannot manipulate them the way we might – moving a book further away or nearer to help us focus on the size of the type, for example. This means that while they can see fine detail well from a distance (better than a cat, in fact), something that has been in their field of vision for some time at close range, might be poorly seen. As it comes into sharp focus at a distance, the horse may then shy at it. This also explains why they can suddenly become transfixed by an object we can barely see, such as someone walking a dog on a hillside several miles away!

SMELL

Horses have an excellent sense of smell and use it extensively. They develop a herd smell on top of their own, which is why a group will often queue up to roll in the same patch of earth when turned out together. It's a bonding ritual which allows them access to that particular 'club', and thus, the greater safety of a herd. Horses greet each other by blowing through the nostrils and it is thought that they can remember another horse's smell ten years after the time they first met. Offering a horse the back of your hand to smell for a couple of seconds is an excellent way of initiating contact and introducing yourself.

Horses also use smell to keep track of their neighbours; this is particularly the case with stallions as they need to know the location and potential dominance of nearby rivals. Stallions will defecate on the droppings of other horses to transmit their own message, and they also use smell to identify mares in season. You may have seen a stallion raising his head and nose, curling up his top lip and closing his nostrils. This is called flehmen, and it draws scent particles over an organ in the roof of the mouth that can detect the smell of a mare on heat. Mares, geldings and foals will also do this when faced with a smell or taste that they don't recognize, such as a herbal treat or other new food. Meanwhile, mares identify their foals almost entirely by scent, which is why fostering an orphan is such a tricky process and entails making the foal smell as much like the mare's real baby as possible.

Horses can smell potential predators as far as 200 metres (600 ft) away on a still day and over a

A RELAXED MOUTH MEANS A RELAXED HORSE

Although it doesn't play as key a role as the eyes and ears, the horse's mouth is also a part of his body language apparatus. The action of a horse's mouth can help tell a rider whether a horse is relaxed and at ease or is apprehensive and tense. The horse that is feeling nervous or uptight about something will move along with his mouth tightly closed. Conversely, the relaxed horse will have eased his jaw muscles and will be working the bit quietly with his tongue.

One of a horse's first indications of relaxation and acceptance of a handler or another horse is when he licks his lips and chews (left). Foals and young horses also use their mouths to signal subservience to older horses. Often, the young horse approaches the older one with his mouth opening and closing, teeth clacking, and tail tucked between his rear legs.

kilometre away when the wind is in the right direction; again, this may lead us to think they are acting strangely for no reason, because we cannot detect these smells. Sensory cells gauge the smell, passing the information to the horse's nervous system and brain, which tell him what the smell means – danger, stranger, water or food, for example. The first horse I ever bought myself was an event horse. Once I got him home and he had settled in, we went off for a hack. He came to a point where he just stopped dead, his head went up, and I could feel his heart beating under me. He became very elevated, and piaffed and passaged down the road. Then we came to a corner and he went like Bambi – front legs slightly splayed, head and neck arched and snorting. I had never encountered anything like it. But, just around that corner was a herd of cows. My horse had smelt them half a

mile down the road, and was terrified of them. In the end, the only way I could get him to cope with cows was to turn him out with just one at a time, building up to two or three then the whole herd. Once he built up his confidence and learned that they moved away from him, he got better.

A strong sense of smell may also explain the horse's uncanny ability to find its way home. Let loose in unfamiliar territory, they tend to travel upwind, rather than directly homeward.

Horses seem particularly sensitive to the smell of water, which is why it's vital to make sure field and stable supplies are fresh. It may also explain why it's so hard to get a horse to drink 'strange' water away from home, or water containing electrolytes. If it's really important for your horse to drink, such as during an endurance event, some nutritionists recommend putting a

couple of drops of peppermint essential oil in the water, to disguise unusual smells.

TASTE

For the horse smell is the essential link to taste. Messages pass along nerves to the brain which then tells the horse what the smell represents, which is why no matter how much you try dressing up bad feed or wormer with apples and molasses, he'll refuse it long before it gets to his mouth.

Saliva is only secreted once the taste buds come into contact with food or some other stimulant. We are conditioned to think that frothing at the mouth is a good sign in the horse, but excessive frothing is actually a sign of distress and may be caused by modern bits with an inbuilt taste that the horse dislikes but which the owner thinks are doing a good job!

TELL-TALE TAIL CARRIAGE

The lofty tail carriage of a horse in flight or showing off is easy enough to see and interpret. As an extension of the spine, it can also tell you a lot about the state of the rest of your horse's back.

A swishing tail may be a sign of irritation, frustration or lack of submission in the ridden horse. A tail stiffly clamped down over the quarters indicates severe discomfort, either physical or mental. A tail that is lifted but with the last vertebrae 'kinked' out of the hair shows insecurity or confusion.

TOUCH

We all know how sensitive a horse is to the lightest touch – they can easily feel a fly landing on their skin for example – and this should always be remembered with a horse that is apparently 'dead' to the aids. Bad riding and poor schooling can mean the horse becomes less responsive as a self-defence mechanism. Yet the horse never looses his ability to feel flies, no matter how badly he has been ridden, which is why reschooling a horse to react to more subtle aids whatever his age is always possible and worthwhile.

The muzzle is the horse's equivalent to our hands and fingers. It is covered with coarse whiskers with many nerve endings in their roots, which act as antennae. Horses are tactile by nature. They explore strange objects on the ground by touching them with a hoof and will frequently touch objects with their nose when smelling them. They often enjoy nudging and rubbing each other and us too.

There is also an inner sense of touch which tells the horse how his body is positioned, when to stale or pass droppings, when he is hungry or thirsty, when he is in pain or simply feels tired or unwell. He can only pass on this information to us by means of his behaviour and demeanour so we must always be prepared to watch closely.

The brain and thinking

Human brains have developed to enable rational thought and work out solutions to problems. This is primarily what is called 'left-brain' thinking, because – to simplify a very complex subject – that is the side of the brain where rational thought takes place, and this is something humans do 80 per cent of the time. **Horses, however, have developed different needs. They don't really need to be rational problem solvers in order to survive in the wild.** All they need is to find food and water and run whenever they sense trouble, and for that they need to be as close to their raw instinct as possible.

Horses use what is called 'right-brain' thinking 80 per cent of the time; this is the type of brain power required for survival in the natural world. Right-brain thinking creates adrenalin, which is agitating, whereas left-brain thinking causes an endorphic release, which is calming.

What I aim to do with this training system is to reverse the use of the horse's right- and left-brain functions, so that he starts to use the left (or rational) side 80 per cent of the time. This will make him think more rationally, stop and analyze instead of bolting off. Why do I want to keep the 20 per cent right-brain reactions?

Well I don't want a robot; I still want to keep the essence of the horse, his personality is important to me. I like a little bit of spark.

Why would I want the horse to think more left-brain at all? The reason is primarily because its what makes him safe to be around and easy to train; using this side will help him analyze the situation rather than taking fright, whipping round and heading for home. Right-brain reactions cancel out any logical thought and so the ability to work things out. It's back to fear, which causes shut down and destroys any thought process.

DEVELOPING LEFT-BRAIN THINKING

Every time you do something 'unnatural' to 'humanize' your horse, such as making him accept tack, walk into the confined space of a trailer or stable, jump brightly coloured showjumps or walk along a road with traffic passing him, you are developing his left-brain thinking. In fact, the very fact he's there at all in a domestic environment means he's come a long way towards the left-brained or human way of thinking.

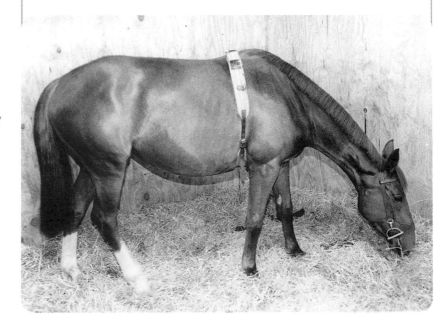

THEY'RE NOT STUPID

Horses are not stupid, they just have different priorities. How often have you accused your horse of being stupid (even if you only muttered it secretly under your breath) or become frustrated at his apparent failure to learn something you're trying to teach him? Saints apart, it's probably happened to most of us at some point in our riding lives, even though deep down we know it's probably our own failure and not the horse's stupidity at all. Consider, though, how quickly even a 'stupid' horse learns to unlatch a gate, open

> The truth is that all horses learn very quickly whenever their behaviour results in a reward, and the bigger the reward, the quicker they will learn.

a feed container or dive out of the arena door, for example! Everyone has a story to tell about great horse escapes and clever ponies. The truth is that all horses learn very quickly whenever their behaviour results in a reward, and the bigger the reward, the quicker they will learn. If a horse manages to open a stable door that allows him out of a poky box into a wide-open space, or a gate from a poached field onto a fresh verge, this is certainly reward enough for him to try that behaviour again. If he can get into the feed room, well, that's definitely worth it! He perfects the art of latch opening by trial and error, not really by 'thinking'.

Sometimes the learned behaviour is less amusing, but it's done for basically the same reason. Take a horse that bucks from physical discomfort for example, and manages to unseat his rider, therefore removing the source of discomfort. Worth a try next time, wouldn't you think? It's not a question of the horse being 'nasty' or 'trying' to get you off. To him, it's a logical route to the comfort zone (and usually the last in a long line of subtle signals and more generous behaviour, such as tail swishing or pinning the ears back, which have been ignored). Take the association one step further, and you might unwittingly 'teach' the horse to hump and buck as he's saddled, before the rider even gets on.

While horses certainly have the raw material in the neocortex of their brain to be capable of thinking, it is

WHY BUCK?

A horse with back pain may discover that by bucking off his rider he eases this pain. However, habitual bucking may also have other causes (see p.144).

WAYS OF LEARNING

Every horse has the 'intelligence' to be trainable, but are you making the most of the raw material? Learning comes in many forms, and some approaches are more effective than others (see also 'Teaching a skill', p.41).

Habituation	*is a simple type of learning where the horse becomes desensitized by being repeatedly exposed to a stimulus that causes him no harm. An example of this is foal imprinting, where the foal is exposed to all manner of harmless stimuli soon after birth such as the sound of clippers, or having fingers in his mouth and ears. In later life, a horse can become used to very heavy traffic or crowds of people waving flags if it is introduced to gradually, and he is never given cause to fear it. The police horse is a master of this art. However, if a horse has had a bad experience that has resulted in him being hurt or threatened by external stimuli, it's a different story. That incredible equine memory, which serves us so well in training, can prove a disadvantage in such instances.*
Classical conditioning	*is when the horse learns to make an association between a particular stimulus and response. For example, when you say 'foot' and tap his foot with a hoofpick to get him to lift his hoof up, or when he comes to the gate at the sound of your car driving into the yard because this heralds the arrival of food.*
Operant conditioning	*is when a horse takes deliberate action either in order to obtain a reward (positive reinforcement) or to avoid something unpleasant (negative reinforcement). For positive reinforcement to be effective, it's important not to give the reward until you see a clear sign of the behaviour you want. With negative reinforcement, it is essential that it is removed the instant the horse acts in an appropriate way. Both positive and negative reinforcement are used to bring a response.*
Punishment	*is quite different from negative reinforcement. It is applied after the horse has acted inappropriately, with the aim of getting rid of a response. Rarely an effective training tool, punishment creates fear, resentment, indecisiveness and other emotional side effects, all of which are contrary to learning. The only time fear is a useful emotion in a horse is when it helps him escape danger.*

more likely to be their instinct to find the most comfortable place in terms of survival that drives their behaviour, and owners often misconstrue this as cleverness. In other words, evolution ensures that every animal adapts to its own niche, which means it develops skills that enable it to solve the problems that threaten its immediate survival. Although we tend to label an animal's problem-solving ability as intelligence, there's little evidence of real analytical ability in horses because they don't have to analyze to survive: they simply need to be hyper-aware of their environment and run as fast as they can when they feel threatened. Conversely, dogs and other predators, which need to think on the move, analyze the unfolding situation and co-operate as hunters in order to bring down their dinner.

> **Although we tend to label an animal's problem-solving ability as intelligence, there's little evidence of real analytical ability in horses because they don't have to analyze to survive: they simply need to be hyper-aware of their environment and run as fast as they can when they feel threatened.**

Early learning

As with humans, the experiences horses have as youngsters influence them greatly in later life. In particular, equine behaviourists believe that traumatic experiences at weaning can set off a chain reaction, resulting in the insecurity and social maladjustment which can cause behavioural problems in later life.

In a domestic situation, weaning is traditionally done when the foal is between four and six months old. A spring-born foal will be approaching six months old in autumn or early winter, when the mare will begin to struggle to provide good quality milk while maintaining her own condition in the absence of lush summer grazing. It's vital for the foal to get the protection of antibodies from their mother's milk in the early days, but after that, most domestic horses are more likely to be overfed than underfed. Foals grow too big, too fast, which causes all kinds of developmental problems and compromises their soundness in later life. If you cut back on the mother's food she can end up looking poor and not supplying all the necessary

nutrients for the foal. Weaning allows the owner to control the diet of both mare and foal much more easily, to the benefit of each.

The method of weaning varies. Some breeders turn mares and foals out in adjoining pastures, which allows them to see, smell and touch each other but prevents nursing. While both mares and foals will probably stand at the fence line for the first week, eventually they lose interest and wander away. Others simply take the mare away, hopefully leaving the foal at least in his familiar surroundings and with the company of other weanlings. This 'cold turkey' method usually involves lots of running around and frantic calling on the part of both mare and foal, and the possibility of injury and

psychological damage is high. Research shows that foals weaned by being removed from their mothers and shut individually in stables were three times more likely to show abnormal behaviour than foals allowed to maintain contact with other foals during weaning, and eight times more likely to show abnormal behaviour than foals not weaned at all.

> **What is the ideal age and method for weaning? Four months, or 120 days, is the lower limit set by the industry, but that's certainly not the time frame nature would choose. In horses, and in humans, cultural rules play a part, and the 'natural' age for self-weaning in the wild is between eight months and one year.**

Without their mother's influence and the gentle reprimands of the rest of the herd, there's the danger that early and heavy-handed weaning leaves youngsters unable to socialize with other horses; it may also lead to separation anxiety, which can cause problems for later handlers and riders. So none of these methods is ideal for the good start in life that we want for our youngsters.

Weaning is, of course, both natural and necessary. In the wild, when a mare becomes pregnant again she will wean her own foal in order to be able to provide sufficient nutrients for the next arrival. She'll do it gradually however, discouraging her offspring from being so reliant with a grimace or harmless kick, with very little stress involved. At the same time, the foal will have less desire to suck because he will be supplementing his diet with grass and other foods.

TEACHING A SKILL

According to behaviourists, training for a new skill should be short, sweet, calm and often, and my experiences certainly support this. Studies show that when trying to teach a horse something, it's the number of trials that are important, not their time, place or duration. The average horse learns something after about six repetitions, but he should be made to do it at least 20 times after which it becomes an automatic response. Called 'overlearning', this ensures that the horse becomes so familiar with the proce-dure, he should remember it even when he becomes nervous or excited. (It's the also psychology behind army drills – doing it again and again in peacetime means that even under the stress of a war-time situation, soldiers can still load their rifles quickly and smoothly.)

This technique implants the skill in the horse's short-term memory; to make the lesson lodge in his long-term memory, the trials should be repeat-ed at least every three days until the process becomes an acquired habit. Hence, while your dearest wish will certainly be to slam up the ramp once you've finally managed to load a difficult horse, the best thing to do is to bring him out again and load him again and again, then do it all over again at least every three days, or until the procedure is habitual.

Failure to understand the necessity for repetition explains why many people succeed, with great difficulty, in getting a horse through a certain procedure one day, reward him, then become frustrated at an apparent lack of progress when they encounter the same old problem a week later. Remember: if you get annoyed or frustrated then the horse tends to focus his attention on this annoyance rather than the task in hand, which ham-pers his learning.

This process of gradual habituation is what we should be trying to emulate at home. Take the time to condition the mare and foal to separation by taking them out of sight of each other, round a corner for example, for just seconds initially, gradually building up to longer periods. Make it fun and comfortable for both parties, perhaps by feeding them both before returning the foal. Teach them that there's no need to panic every time they are parted, because they'll soon see each other again. By taking a little time and being sympathetic at this stage, you'll be doing all you can to produce a horse without hang-ups.

Testing the system

For a long time I had wanted to put what I knew about training to the test, and as I have never been around a horse from the day it was born right through to early adult life, I decided I was going to breed two foals as my 'control' group. I decided on two so that the foals could be weaned together. I had two nice mares. Patsy is a very dominant ex-racehorse; if I had got her early enough she would have been a fantastic eventer. I put her to Welton Crackerjack. The other mare, Lilly, was a youngster who didn't really trust people very much and had had a few bad experiences in the first two years of her life. I put her to my stallion, Nosey, who is from a fantastic eventing line but, through no fault of his own, had become unrideable. With work we did manage to ride him but he never really enjoyed it; his temperament is so fantastic in every other respect that I didn't want to push the issue, so he is now turned out and is visited by the odd mare or two.

I waited for my foals with bated breath. Patsy was the first to give birth, to a stunning colt that we named Fly-by-Night. For about ten minutes after he was born I imprinted him, which was the most fantastic experience, with his mum watching from a foot away. She is normally very domineering and possessive, but on that occasion she looked calm and totally unworried by the situation. About four weeks later Lilly had a lovely chestnut filly that we named Scarlet, mainly because she was so red but also because she behaved like a 'scarlet woman' with Fly. I also imprinted Scarlet.

WEANING

Weaning Scarlet and Fly was so uneventful that I don't really remember it. It always helps when there are two foals, but also because they were used to coming in and doing some work as individuals, they became quite independent of each other. They shared a stable for the first winter and had been turned out with each other since the day they were born, yet I could still take them away from each other to work without either of them suffering any form of separation anxiety.

HABITUATION

Habituation is a simple type of learning where the horse becomes desensitized by being repeatedly exposed to a stimulus that causes him no harm, as my Thoroughbred yearling Fly demonstrates here

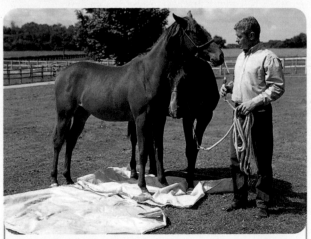

REASSURANCE IN NUMBERS

Horses have a strong social structure and gain huge reassurance from the presence of other horses. It makes sense to use this in your training to build confidence and clarify communication. Here, my two youngsters Scarlet and Fly see the plastic tarpaulin as an interesting game to play together, rather than a frightening obstacle that must be faced alone.

EARLY DAYS

Over the next three years I would periodically bring them in from the field and work with them. I halter trained them at quite a young age, and did just a few bits here and there, such as walking over a large see-saw (right).

Getting them to accept tack was not really an issue after this kind of preparation and when it came to preparing them for backing, I did a lot of leading them off an older more experienced horse.

I face the same pressures as anyone else in trying to fit my horses around work, family and social pressures, but in spite of only getting ridden for 15–20 minutes 3–4 times a week, they are both, without a shadow of a doubt, the easiest and best-behaved horses I have ever dealt with. Obviously I am a little biased, but when the time came for me to find them new homes where they could do the jobs they were bred for, every potential purchaser, without exception, commented on their good manners. They are still cheeky with bags of personality, but this doesn't have to mean rude!

The other side of a good early learning experience is that it creates a bond between you and your youngster without going down the road of over familiarity, which always does breed contempt in my opinion – what's funny when the foal is three months old is not funny when it is three years old. Not only will you create a great bond with this way of training but you will also have a young horse that is obedient for the farrier, vet and anyone else he comes into contact with. You will also have the most well-behaved foal at any show, because he will be content to walk and trot at your shoulder without any messing about. If you have taken it a step further you will have trained your mare at the same time; with Lilly this really helped her confidence and she now is very comfortable around people. And ultimately, you're doing your horse a big favour. Circumstances can change no matter how unlikely it may seem in the early days, and should either you or he have to move on for any reason, you're far more likely to find him a good home where he will be loved and valued if his education has turned him into something loving and valuable!

SEE-SAW SOLUTION

Using the 'see-saw' helped Scarlet and Fly with loading and it also taught them that if they shifted their weight they could control what happened with the see-saw. It made them think about what they were doing, encouraging them to use the left side of the brain. They also became used to walking over plastic and tarpaulin sheets, getting so blasé about the whole thing that eventually they would pick the sheet up and play with it.

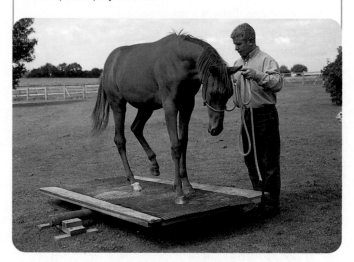

FOLLOW MY LEADER

Leading my youngsters off a more experienced horse was excellent for their confidence but it also got them used to me sitting above them so when I eventually got on them, it was the most uneventful day! It was just a logical progression, and they didn't even think about getting rid of me. As three year olds, they hacked out happily on their own.

The mechanics of ground training

As explained, **my system relies on the horse's natural desire to move from discomfort to an area of comfort,** and is based on the horse's own method of communication through visual, tactile and emotional pressure.

Pressure can come in various forms, and what the horse must learn is that his answer must remain the same – respect it, give it your attention and move away, whether it's from a hand gesture (visual pressure), halter, rope, rein or leg (tactile pressure). Whenever the horse responds, he is rewarded by a release of that pressure and maybe a little extra to make it really worth his while, such as a pat. It's as simple as that.

In Ground Training from a Distance (pp.54–81) you'll see how emotional pressure comes into play in training the ridden horse using rope

> Something that will really upset your horse is inconsistency. The major thing to remember when training horses is that it isn't how quickly you put the pressure on that impresses them, but how quickly you take it off.

circling and long lining. For now, we'll concentrate on teaching the horse the basics through physical pressure, using a pressure halter. As he becomes more attentive, many of the physical cues will become unnecessary and he should begin to respond to much more subtle visual cues as shown.

EQUIPMENT

I use a training halter and a selection of ropes in all my work (see below).

The point of a training halter is not to put pressure on a horse so you can drag him about or be severe on him, but to use pressure as a training aid. One of the key points when we are training horses is for them to be able to separate our 'Yes' from our 'No'. If we apply pressure and the horse makes the tiniest move in the right direction, we must *immediately* release the pressure. In this way we can enable the horse to learn what is expected of him really quickly. Something that will really upset your horse is inconsistency. Think back to what I said about my teachers (p.29)! The major thing to remember when training horses is that it isn't how quickly you put the pressure on that

TRAINING HALTER

There are numerous designs of pressure halter on the market, but I found most to be unsatisfactory, so I designed and now manufacture my own from slippery braid-on-braid yachting rope, which never sticks. So many so-called pressure halters (or maybe they are aptly named as that is exactly what they do) put pressure on but never release it; the handler has to step forward to release the pressure, which means that the horse doesn't understand – the reward comes too late. (Suitable pressure halters can be purchased from me, see p.149, or any reputable natural horsemanship association, such as those set up by Pat Parelli or Monty Roberts.)

impresses them, but how quickly you take it off.

Remember this pressure and release ('yes' and 'no') system works right the way through your horsemanship. For example, if you want a half halt, apply a little pressure to the reins, and as the horse responds immediately release the pressure. This will give your horse a payoff for his actions and he will become light and responsive to you. Practise giving your horse the lightest signal to start with and see if you can get a response from that first. If not you can always apply a little more pressure.

Remember, too, that if you are rough in your handling of your horse, you can damage your relationship with him using any halter, including a normal head collar.

FIRST STEPS

The basic principle of pressure and release affects every area of your horse's life and your relationship with him, from basic manners in the stable to advanced competition. If he moves quickly and easily away from pressure (or better, the mere anticipation of pressure) on the ground, he will be well on the way to understanding more complex and subtle ridden aids at a later stage of his training. That is why you owe it to the horse, particularly a youngster, to spend the time teaching him from the ground and this will subsequently minimize the stress and discomfort of having a rider on board later. You'll also make life much easier for yourself!

When asking your horse questions like those outlined below, you are in fact asking him to use the left side of his brain. He has to think about what

ROPES AND LONG LINES

This is a selection of the ropes I use. From right to left: a thick, heavy rope of around 2.5m (8ft) for close work, a thinner 4m (12ft) for rope circling and a very thin 15m (50ft) rope to move on to as the horse's obedience builds up to a point where you can test it at a greater distance. Two long lines of identical length (10m/32ft) and weight are also shown.

you are asking and then come up with an answer. This causes an endorphic release, which, if you watch him closely, you will see will start to make him sleepy, so keep the sessions relatively short, say 5–10 minutes for a young horse and 10–15 minutes for an older horse. And remember ground training isn't about naughty horses but about adding variety to and improving your ridden work.

The lessons described here need to be done on both sides of the horse. You'll have to start from scratch and teach each lesson afresh on each side. Horses do not easily

transfer a lesson they have learned on one side to the other, and their response may also alter if they find it more physically demanding or difficult to co-ordinate themselves on one side compared to the other. And, why not? The percentage of ambidextrous people in the world is tiny, and it's the same with horses!

With any of the exercises in this book, always work in a safe environment, where your horse can feel relaxed and there are not too many distractions. A small paddock or menage is ideal. Never start work if you are tired or in a bad mood or short of time.

STEP-BY-STEP GUIDE TO HALTER TRAINING

With any young horse, or one that is new to you, it's essential to start here, even if you think you're stating the obvious to him. By all means move quickly through this part of the programme, if it's clear that your horse understands the principles – but you'll be surprised how many don't, even those that appear to be well schooled, then you discover that there are large gaps in the foundations, which crumble as the training becomes more advanced! A little test to try is to see whether your horse steps back from the slightest pressure on the halter. If he doesn't then he does not truly understand to move away from pressure.

Introduce pressure and release. The simplest way to introduce the horse to the idea of pressure and release is to start with a rope halter. Pressure is put on the horse's nose and poll, and released the moment he stops resisting and steps in the direction you're asking. He is doubly rewarded for his co-operation, firstly by instant release of the pressure and secondly with praise from the handler. It is his movement towards you that will release the pressure.

1 You can see that Troy resists the pressure at first, but I remain passive. This is important: the exercise is not about forcing him or pulling him towards me. Simply apply the pressure and wait for him to work out what he needs to do to make life easy for himself. When you first start this work, stand very close to the horse, so that a single step will bring him to you at first, then gradually increase the distance (ie the rope length) between you as he gets the idea.

2 Do not be tempted to step towards him – this is about getting attention, focus and respect, so make him come to you. If he starts moving backwards, follow him maintaining the same pressure until he figures out that this will not release the pressure.

3 As you can see (inset, far right), he soon finds that responding to my simple request is a fast route back to the comfort zone, where he rewarded.

...how you teach the basic principles of pressure and release

Gain quarter control. These may be simple techniques, but remember there's a serious purpose behind them all. The aim is that this training will eventually produce a horse that is light, balanced and more responsive under saddle. Once your horse has started to grasp the pressure-release idea, your next step is to gain control of his quarters.

1 Apply the same pressure-release principle to his back end. In other words, ask them to move away from pressure, initially by spinning the rope near his quarters, not touching them. Keep the halter contact slack.

2 As before, the moment the horse makes the right decision, reward him for his co-operation by ceasing to apply the pressure (stop spinning the rope). It's essential that you make it very clear to him which is the right movement, for which he will be rewarded, so it he knows exactly what he needs to do. To do this you need to be completely consistent in your own behaviour and quietly persist in asking him to move his quarters away from you, until he does so.

There is no penalty or punishment as such for the 'wrong' movement, or indeed no movement at all – other than your quietly persistent pressure, which will irritate (but not hurt or frighten) him into making the right move. This is about presenting the horse with a 'win-win' situation, making him an offer so simple and so obviously to his own benefit, that he can't refuse! Remember horses will always choose the path of least resistance.

Reduce the pressure. When I go back to this exercise in a later session, after just a few moments spent using the rope to apply tactile pressure to his quarters, Troy begins responding to visual pressure (a simple hand gesture) by moving his quarters accordingly. When the horse begins to understand and anticipate what you are asking, it should be unnecessary to touch him. Tone down your signals until they are as subtle as you can get while still achieving a response.

HALTER TRAINING (continued)

Get shoulder control. Now it's time to move to the front end, starting by manoeuvring the shoulders in the same way as the quarters. Control of the shoulders is the key to a horse being light and obedient under saddle, and for resolving myriad ridden problems such as spooking and napping; it also tackles the majority of handling problems, which invariably arise when the horse has learned to use his shoulder against you. Think about it – if your horse naps, he does it through his shoulder; if he rears, it's evasion through the shoulder; when he runs out at a fence? yep, it's evasion through the shoulder.

1 Start by spinning the rope at the shoulders until the horse reads the signal and moves them away, reward by easing the pressure and praising as before.

2 As lessons progress, once the horse starts to understand and anticipate what you want, the rope spinning will become too crude a signal. See how subtle you can get *while still getting a response*. You want to reward the horse for his co-operation by being quieter and more polite with your commands, but it's no good toning them down to a level where he finds it easy to ignore you.

3 Aim to reach a stage where you can simply step towards him or gesture at his shoulder (right) to get him to step away from you.

Back up. Backing up a horse on the ground is a very useful exercise, both physically and psychologically. It's particularly important for a horse that is any way pushy or bargy. Apply the pressure-release principle as before, asking for a step back then releasing the pressure when you get it.

…building on the basic principles of pressure and release

G et subtle. Remember to keep putting your work to the test by seeing how little you have to do to get a response from your horse. You're aiming to get your signals as subtle as possible. When the horse is reading your body language rather than waiting for physical stimuli, you've reached a higher plane of communication.

1 Here, I start by applying direct physical pressure to ask Troy to back up.

2 Then as Troy begins to understand, I can reduce this until there is no physical pressure at all and he is backing up on a loose rope purely in response to my body language, which is positive with my shoulders square on.

3 I make sure that I walk with a strong and positive rhythm, this produces the same action in him.

...starting on advanced movements

Advanced movements. Once you have got the horse's concentration and have laid the basic foundations, practise manoeuvring his body around in different ways. These exercises are of enormous gymnastic benefit, developing physical strength and dexterity.

1 A simple hand signal asks Troy to execute a turn on the forehand, moving his quarters away from me.

2 Shoulder in (below left) is achieved by using visual pressure to ask Troy to move forward while still maintaining control of his shoulders.

3 Here is turn on the haunches. We do the exercises on both sides, so Troy knows exactly what I want.

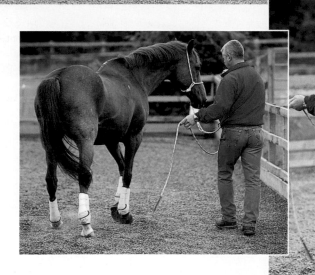

4 By the end of the day Troy is really starting to get the message to move away – wherever the pressure comes from or whatever form it takes, whether it's from the rope; the handler's body language, or a finger on the nose or hand on the face, as shown here.

...the benefits of having a well-mannered horse

Increasing responsiveness. Here's an example of how this basic pressure-release training will contribute to a well-mannered ridden horse.

1 I am asking this horse to lower his head in response to pressure.

2 He does as I ask and I reward him with a rub and a release of pressure.

3 From here it's a short step to teaching him that when he feels pressure in his mouth from the bit (below).

4 He should take the action necessary to relieve it, that is drop his head (bottom). What a pleasure it is to have a horse this responsive to the slightest rein contact!

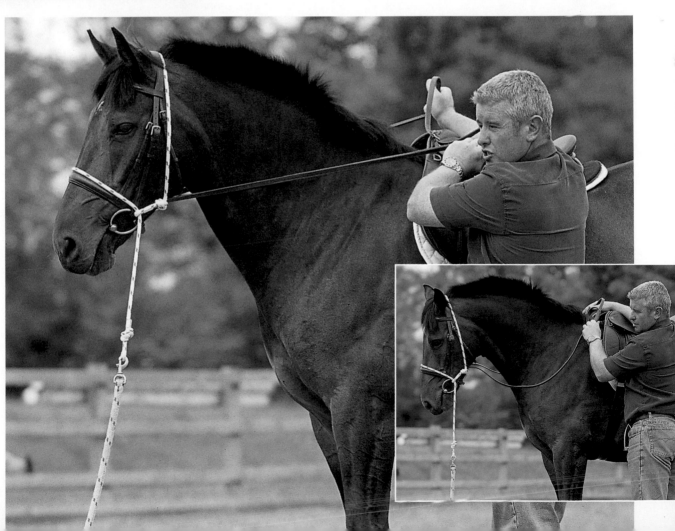

...who needs a rope?

Have fun. This training isn't all about going through boring drills in the school. Once you can drive your horse's quarters with a gesture, control his shoulders and trust him to give to even light pressure, you can use these skills to further his training and gymnastic development in all sorts of other ways.

There's no reason why a young horse shouldn't occasionally be participating in this type of exercise (right) from as young as six months. (See pp.90–91, for more on how to progress and prepare a horse's ridden work using the pressure halter.)

Who needs a rope? Remember, less is more when it comes to equine communication, so practise letting go once the horse has grasped the basics.

1 This horse is happy to oblige without being 'tied' to me. The idea that to be close to me is the most comfortable place is so strongly confirmed in his mind that the link between us has become mental rather than physical.

2 This mental 'rope', often referred to as 'join-up', has been widely shown as something of a party trick in recent years. It is not an end in itself; it simply demonstrates that the horse's mental focus and attention is entirely upon me

3 Here (inset) he is making a totally free choice to respond to me by jumping over the log.

Tips for getting off to a good start

Breaking and training, or retraining, a horse can seem like a huge task. What you need is a programme that guides you through it bit by bit, just like studying for an exam or learning another language. Start with the basics and only move on when you are sure your horse understands everything and when you and he have been successful at each earlier stage. This is how you build a firm foundation.

▷ Have a plan – every journey needs a start and finish point (otherwise how will you know how far you have to go or even when you've got there?) and a good map for in between.

▷ Break the 'journey' down into manageable chunks that fit with your life, time, facilities and other resources.

▷ If you get a bit stuck or things don't go according to plan, go back a step to where you were both comfortable before trying to move on again. Begin each session by repeating the successful steps from last time before starting a new lesson.

▷ Beware of rewarding too soon or expecting too little – it may slow down your progress. Imagine the example of a difficult loader. He gets almost to the top of the ramp then stops. Thinking that she is bound to get him in now, his excited owner gives him a treat – but then he'll go no further. In fact, he may start backing down the ramp again. Reward only what constitutes actual progress from the previous time, that means successful completion of the particular 'chunk' you had planned for that day, however small.

▷ Respect your horse's intelligence and individuality. Although there is no scientific data to back it up, many animal behaviourists, riders and trainers agree that the naughtiest individuals are often also the most intelligent and talented! While these horses may prove to be the most difficult to handle, they can also be expected to learn or relearn good habits quickly. Likewise, recognizing a slower learner is essential to successful training.

▷ Don't get sidetracked or allow the horse to make you angry or emotional – no matter what happens, remember the three basic points you have to convey to him are: that the procedure doesn't really hurt (and make sure that this is, indeed, the case); ordinary resistance or reasonable reaction will not stop the procedure (use the minimum restraint necessary for everyone's safety); and compliance will lead to a reward (this does not mean that non-compliance will be punished).

Key lessons to take forward

▷ Whoever controls movement and direction is in charge, so make sure it's you! Practise manoeuvring the horse's quarters and shoulders to get forward, backwards and sideways movement.

▷ Make sure you've got his mental focus too by keeping the exercises varied and sessions short, with lots of reward for the right response. As you may have experienced yourself at work, reward and enthusiasm from your manager is very motivating, while constant negative feedback and having your efforts ignored has the opposite effect!

▷ Start with tactile pressure and refine it until he is responding to largely visual cues. Subtlety and lightness in your 'aids' from the ground will translate to your ridden work.

▷ It's vital that the horse associates good behaviour with instant reward, which means releasing the pressure (in whatever form it takes) the moment you get a response, even if the response is not as quick or pronounced as you'd hoped. By asking for more even when he's done as you asked, you're nagging him unfairly and blurring the lines between right and wrong. His generosity and motivation to give more will improve with understanding and practice. This is the beginning of ground training from a distance, which is your next step.

2 Ground training from a distance

Why train from the ground?

By now you should have a horse that understands the principles of pressure and release, is attuned to watching your body language and is starting to develop more co-ordination and motivation in his work. However, it's all very well moving your horse around when you're standing next to him, but does he still listen when you're at a distance – at the end of a lunge line, for example?

There are two good reasons why you should develop obedience from afar, or distance learning, in your horse. One is because when you're riding him, you're effectively communicating from a distance. It's also a sign of his respect for you and a test of his true understanding when he will carry out what you ask when you're not physically guiding him through it step-by-step. The second reason is because it's necessary for you to back off, physically and mentally, in order to allow the horse to work in his own energy and balance and for you to observe him as he does so. In other words, to develop the self-carriage he needs to be a light, balanced and responsive ride, you need to step back and see what happens rather than being on hand all the time just in case he falters, thus stalling the learning process.

SELF-CARRIAGE – WHAT IT IS AND WHY YOUR HORSE NEEDS IT

A lot of emphasis is placed on the position of the horse's head and neck when schooling. Over the years, phrases such as 'long and low', 'up and collected' or 'working deep' have been overused, abused and misunderstood. This has led to them losing their true meaning. Instead, try to think of having a horse that can hold and control his own body weight in perfect balance, on both reins and at all paces, with or without a rider – this is self-carriage.

Many riders know the end result they want, but not the means to get it. However, the principles of teaching a horse lightness and self-carriage are much more simple than you think, and the route to them is in your groundwork.

By asking your horse to carry himself during the rope circling and long reining exercises described in the following pages, you will prepare him physically for the ridden work during which he will be expected not only to carry his own weight but also that of the rider.

At first he will find this work difficult but don't be tempted to add a gadget even though this will immediately make him look prettier. It is an illusion! As soon as you remove the gadget, he will revert to his old way of going. Instead, persist with laying solid and permanent foundations, which will make it easy for the horse to stay light, engaged, balanced and forward, even with the additional weight of a rider. The result? A 'virtuous' circle – the horse feels physically comfortable and capable of doing as he is asked, and has learnt to respond immediately to subtle pressure, so the rider can give minimal aids and enjoy the ride without interfering. For me, this is the true meaning of 'dressage'.

WHERE DOES DRESSAGE COME IN?

Dressage may be a competitive sport, but first and foremost it is a form of gymnastic training, a series of exercises designed to teach the horse to use his body correctly so he can carry out his work more efficiently and develop the impression of harmony and lightness between horse and rider. As well as the physical aims, dressage is about increasing understanding and co-operation between horse and rider, and devoting time to learning to ride better.

Whatever level you're at, dressage is basically a test of how well a horse carries himself, summed up as his 'way of going'. If the horse is using his body in a way that is biomechanically efficient and appropriate for his stage of training, then he is in a good outline. Whether this is the longer, lower outline of a horse that is in the process of learning to carry itself better, or the higher, collected frame of an advanced horse, which has developed that ability through years of training, doesn't really matter.

These two extremes represent the beginning and end of the long and complex journey that is horse training, and the myriad different outlines in between simply show which stage of the journey you are at.

How does a horse move?

Before we can expect to achieve self-carriage (see pp.56–57) we must understand how the horse uses his body, so we know what is possible for him, what is not and why, and how certain exercises can help or hinder what we are trying to teach him.

> In his ECONOMICAL state, the horse is heavy on the ground, difficult to guide and stop; riding him is jarring and uncomfortable and he is apt to stumble.
>
> In his EXTRAVAGANT state, he is very light and responsive and literally dances over the ground in a beautifully balanced way.

The horse has two different gymnastic states – the state of economy, which has evolved from years of being an efficient forager wandering vast distances expending as little energy as possible, and the state of extravagance, when that same horse parades himself with maximum lift and energy, covering very little ground. In other words, he has one image for every day use and another he reserves for special occasions! Our riding experience will be equally extreme, depending on which gymnastic state the horse is displaying.

In his economical state, the horse is heavy on the ground, difficult to guide and stop; riding him is jarring and uncomfortable and he is apt to stumble. Stumbling is indicative of a horse that is out of balance, whether it's with or without a rider. The unbalanced horse is always relying on the rider to support it, and when this

doesn't happen, it can become uncomfortable and even unsafe to ride since it is effectively missing its 'fifth leg'. As a rider, you can tell if a horse is used to being 'propped up' because he will feel heavy in the hand. (We'll focus more on this and how to avoid it in Making the Connection to Ridden Work, pp.82–113, see also p.129.)

In his extravagant state, he is very light and responsive and dances over the ground. His muscles are braced to carry him, relieving the skeleton of its supportive function and reducing shock on the limbs. If we can encourage him to carry himself in this way on a regular basis, his ability to maintain such a state will improve and as a result he will be physically sounder, more beautiful to look at and a greater pleasure to ride. This is our schooling aim, and it is as much for the horse's health as for our own benefit.

SCHOOLING

Schooling is the process of encouraging the horse to change his posture from economical to extravagant, or to use a more familiar phrase – to develop his

> **EXTRAVAGANT STATE**
>
> *A horse working in his extravagant state is in perfect balance and is a great pleasure to ride.*

A BALANCED HORSE

Long lining teaches a horse to lengthen the distance between withers and poll and achieve balance by carrying himself.

ability to collect. There are plenty of short cuts that will result in the horse tucking his nose into his chest, which can give the impression that he is 'working well' to those who have the head and neck position as their main focus. However, what many riders either forget or never learn is that pulling the horse's head in does not result in self-carriage. What you should be trying to achieve is a lengthening of the distance between the withers and the poll, not a shortening of the distance between the chin and the chest. A balanced horse will naturally carry himself in this way, and this is where long lining is so valuable, as it teaches him to adopt such an outline and therefore develop self-carriage.

Whatever your schooling process, it should have one simple aim, and that's to stimulate the horse to engage good posture thus helping him to develop self-carriage and become physically able to maintain it for longer periods. Engaged postural muscles and good balance enjoy a cause and effect relationship: if a horse has engaged postural muscles he will display good balance. This is also true in reverse.

TRAINING POSTURE

A really talented horse is one that, among other qualities, has a natural tendency to engage his 'postural ring' and hold himself correctly. Most horses have to be taught to do this. (The 'postural ring' refers to a

A CROOKED HORSE

Among other evasions that he developed in order to cope with the demands that were made on him in his youth, Troy learnt to move crookedly. However, even though he is now in his teens, he can still learn about self-carriage which in turn will improve his performance (see also pp.134–137, 140–141).

number of consecutive and interconnecting muscles that run from the horse's poll, over his back, down the back of each hind quarter, under the belly and up through his front legs to his throat. These are the muscles which need to be correctly activated if the horse is to carry himself with lightened forehand, lifted back, contracted stomach muscles and lowered haunches.)

Muscles have a 'memory' which means that they unconsciously fall into a groove worn with repetition. When this groove is not the correct one, then you (or your horse) have picked up a bad habit. This might reveal itself in your horse being strung-out and hollow, or one-sided. Symptoms of imbalance are an irregular rhythm and a tendency to

fall left or right off the chosen line. Luckily, with practice and concentration, it's perfectly possible to re-programme muscle memory into maintaining a good habit. Rather like someone telling you to keep your shoulders back and stop slouching, you need to keep gently reminding your horse to engage his postural ring and encourage him to adopt the new posture.

By regulating the rhythm and preventing the horse from falling in or out on circles and straight lines, we have the first key to self-carriage. If we can then ignite the horse's energies and induce him to maintain a lively activity without chasing him then we have the second key – impulsion. Lastly, if we can teach him to accept the bridle in a way that stretches the nuchal ligament along

the top of the neck and contracts the muscles from under the neck though to the abdominal muscles which lift the back, then we have the third key.

The whole mechanism will fall naturally into place.

Groundwork is the starting point from which to develop the horse's mental and physical ability to do all these things and you can later transfer these lessons to your ridden work (see pp.82–113).

UNDERSTANDING MUSCLES

Different types of muscle fibre have different properties. Some muscles (postural) are designed to hold you in place for long periods of time without tiring, others (locomotor) are designed to produce blasts of energy for immediate movement which they can only keep up for limited periods. So, you remain upright all day without being conscious of your back muscles holding you there, but if you are, say, shifting heavy sacks, a different type of muscle is needed and it can only work for limited time before having to be rested.

An unschooled horse will use mainly locomotor muscles to hold himself up when he is ridden. These tire quickly and can become sore. The purpose of schooling is to engage the postural muscles so they can fulfil the function that they were designed for and liberate the locomotor muscles for their primary function – that of sustaining unimpeded movement.

Your horse's behaviour is an indication of his physical threshold – if he becomes 'bored', naughty or loses concentration after 15 minutes, it's likely to be because he's reached his physical limit and is fidgeting out of discomfort.

FEEL IT YOURSELF

Imagine you are giving a child a play horseback ride. What happens when you hollow your back? Your neck naturally wants to 'crick' at the base and your face comes up. You could force yourself to bring your head back down while keeping your back hollow, but only a limited amount and with great difficulty while clamping your jaw and throat. At the same time, your 'quarters' probably feel like they are being pushed out behind you. If you wanted to bring your knee forward right underneath your belly button ('engage' in horse terms), you'd find it physically almost impossible. And how does the weight of the child on your back make you feel? Pretty uncomfortable and about to slip a disc at any minute!

Now lift your back, rounding up to meet the weight of the child. You'll notice you actually use your stomach muscles to do this, not your back muscles at all. And what happens to your head and neck? They want to continue the curve of the spine and drop down, drawing your 'quarters' underneath you in a natural and relaxed way. Now that child can bounce about a fair amount without causing you much discomfort.

Bear this in mind next time you're schooling your horse – if the horse has been allowed to develop correct self-carriage rather than forced into an 'outline', his back will be up and his neck and head will be down and his quarters will be able to step under and engage without any 'help' (strong leg or hand) from the rider.

A CORRECT OUTLINE

▷ *helps the horse carry his rider in the most efficient and comfortable way.*

▷ *depends on the horse's age and level of training.*

▷ *is the result of a chain of events that starts with the horse lifting his back, a by-product of which is a rounded neck and lowered head.*

▷ *positions the vertebrae in such a way as to allow movement and bending.*

▷ *helps the horse transfer his body weight back on to his haunches (sometimes referred to as 'collection').*

▷ *is necessary for the horse's comfort, balance, impulsion and gymnastic development. In turn, this maintains and enhances the purity of the paces.*

▷ *(Little Pelo has learnt how to work in the correct outline without the use of artificial aids, or even a bit.)*

A BAD OUTLINE

▷ *causes discomfort.*

▷ *impedes balance, impulsion and correct gymnastic development (leading to physical problems that result in disunited canter, difficulty in striking off on the correct lead, favoured diagonal in trot, and so on).*

▷ *leads to incorrect or unorthodox movement, which is damaging to the horse's muscular and skeletal structure. Correct movement is therapeutic, restorative and developmental. So you owe it to your horse to develop his self-carriage whether or not you're interested in competitive dressage, because that way he'll stay sounder for longer.*

▷ *can still look nice! But 'fiddling' your horse into a pretty outline is the equivalent of building your house on weak foundations, and does him no favours in the long run for all the reasons already mentioned. The horse is often an obliging partner in crime, since working incorrectly can require less effort in the early stages. But you will both be found out eventually!*

▷ *(Although not perfect, Troy's outline here is a great improvement on earlier attempts.)*

Developing self-carriage

So, how can we make the horse's life easier by engaging the postural muscles and developing self-carriage before we even mount? By using rope circling and long lining.

ROPE CIRCLING

Rope circling is different to lungeing because it's more interactive, stimulating the horse's mind as well as his body. In circling you are constantly asking your horse to move away and then come back, focusing on you for the next instruction. In lungeing you get your horse to go out on a circle and stay there; it is generally far too reliant on the whip, to which the horse becomes either dull or over-reactive. The other great value of rope circling is that changes of direction need no fiddling or changes of equipment or position from the handler.

The process of changing direction in rope circling is an excellent test of how closely the horse is listening to you. Because he has learned to shift his quarters away from pressure and turn to face the handler in response to a gesture to the quarters, he is in an ideal position to watch for the signal indicating the direction the handler wants him to go in next. An open arm pointing in the direction required, backed up by rope spinning towards the shoulders to drive the horse away only when required, should be more than sufficient.

When practising rope circling, use frequent changes of pace and direction to keep the horse's attention and work on improving his balance and co-ordination. See 'Controls for long lining' (p.73) for hints on getting transitions and stopping.

TRAINING TIPS

▷ *Once you ask the horse to move away from you and start circling on the rope or line, he must continue until he receives his next instruction. At first he's likely to stop every time you remove the pressure, but don't try preventing him making that mistake by applying continual pressure. The learning process comes about through allowing mistakes to happen so that you can correct them.*

So when the horse stops doing as he is asked, for example trotting round you on the circle, calmly put him back to work again. Gradually the number of corrections necessary will become fewer, and he will start correcting himself before you get the chance!

▷ *Don't push your luck or the horse's generosity by asking too much. Set him up to succeed and feel good about himself, not to fail. This is the way to create a self-motivated and content animal.*

STEP-BY-STEP GUIDE TO ROPE CIRCLING

Introduce the concepts. Before starting rope circling make sure your horse understands the principles of pressure and release (see pp.44–52), by assessing her response to the pressure on the halter. This mare overreacts at first, but soon picks up on what is required.

1 The first exercise is essentially about taking control of direction and movement for all the reasons already explained – to establish yourself as the decision maker of the 'herd' and to gain the horse's focus, attention and respect. I make it easier for this horse to work out what I want by sending her quarters away with a spin of the rope (below), thus bringing her head naturally around to face me for her reward.

2 Within just a few minutes of starting, I have this mare's full attention (below). Look at her left ear registering my command for her to move in that direction. I signal what I want by applying visual pressure to her right shoulder through swinging the rope (this can be backed up with tactile pressure with the end of the rope on her shoulder if she fails to respond) while indicating that the 'door' is open to allow her movement to the left.

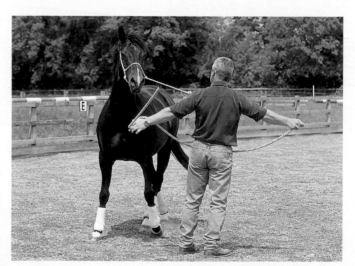

3 OK, so we get another over-reaction (left). At least it shows that the mare is watching me very carefully now, ready to spring into action at my slightest command. Since I am staying calm and neither punishing nor rewarding her for this behaviour, she will soon work out that she is the only one working hard here, and that she is actually making life difficult for herself! This is simply another form of evasion and it will get her nowhere.

...how you teach the basic principles of rope circling

4 Secure in the knowledge that the mare understands the concept of pressure and release, I apply pressure to the line to draw her head to me, which naturally has the effect of sending her quarters away. Compare this to the wilful display in the first picture (left). Now the mare's demeanour is much more humble and she is really concentrating on me. Even though I am several feet away, she is careful not to allow the rope to tighten while waiting for her next instruction. Note that when I reward her, I will bring her to me by shortening the line, not by walking towards her.

5 Altogether calmer, the mare has quickly learnt that there was no benefit in the decision to run she made earlier. Note also that there is no tension in the line. Horses quickly become so attuned to avoiding pressure on the halter that you should be able to circle them just with fingertips. This is the beginning of teaching them self-balance, as well as obedience from a distance; this mare is learning not to lean, a concept she will eventually carry through to her ridden work.

6 Clearly there are no hard feelings here! The lesson has been learnt to such a degree that by the end of this session, which lasted about 15 minutes, the mare is choosing not to exercise her 'right to run' and continues to acknowledge that I am in charge of movement and direction, even without a rope. Sometimes known as 'join-up', this is a sign that you have your horse's respect, focus and attention and is a good indicator that you are ready to move on. It is not an end in itself, however, and if it doesn't happen, it's not the end of the world!

ROPE CIRCLING (continued)

The sequence of photographs shown here and on pp.68–69 is an example of how you can progress the rope circling work to test your skills and ability to command the horse's focus, respect and obedience from an ever-

> Most of us habitually try to manhandle our horses, even when doing something as simple as leading them in from the field. Let go of that lead rope clip and you may be surprised to see that nothing happens other than the horse dropping his head in relief and walking in a relaxed way alongside you!

increasing distance. Psychologically, it's also a very important lesson for the handler, as most of us are terrible at letting go and tend to be in the habit of crowding our horses as if we expect them to misbehave. (As if we stood the faintest hope of stopping them physically if they did!) Most of us habitually try to manhandle our horses, even when doing something as simple as leading them in from the field. Let go of that lead rope clip and you may be surprised to see that nothing happens, other than the horse dropping his head in relief and walking in a relaxed way alongside you! If not then you've only been masking the problem anyway, and until you acknowledge it, you can't get rid of it.

These exercises should give you the confidence to let go and realize that the answer does not lie in the strength of your hands. Imagine the benefits (and relief to your horse) of learning to 'keep your distance' in this way in your ridden work too! Be honest, if you knotted your reins and let your arms hang by your sides as you rode, how many times a minute would you be dying to grab or at least 'tweak' them as you carried out your schooling, instead of exploring more subtle ways of communicating with your horse? That's an exercise worth trying in a safe environment on a sensible horse – I'm pretty sure you'll be horrified at your reliance on manual control. How will your horse learn to respond to a whisper if all you ever do is shout? Indeed, how will you know if he already responds to a whisper, if you keep shouting anyway?

ROPE DRAG

Remember one practical point, it's very important that you choose rope of a lighter weight as you increase the distance between you and your horse, so that the weight of the rope does not put undue pressure on the halter and demotivate the horse.

The weight of the rope alone can be enough to create 'drag' and therefore halter pressure on a horse that is attuned to this system. In order to avoid this, as I increase the length of rope, to increase the distances involved in my ground training, I also use thinner and lighter rope.

...increasing the distance

Reiterate the ground rules. This is my own horse, Little Pelo, and even with a horse as experienced as he is I always spend a few minutes confirming the basics at the beginning of a groundwork session. You don't need to spend ages going over old ground – this is supposed to be a quick, stimulating and user-friendly way of working your horse! Just a quick run through of pressure-release, forward (below left), back (left), left and right (below), to remind him of who is responsible for movement and direction and to give him an idea of where today's session is coming from.

ROPE CIRCLING (continued)

Move out. All these exercises should now be looking familiar.

1 We're now working on a 15m (50ft) line but the techniques remain the same and Pelo understands perfectly what is required.

2 I use visual pressure to move Pelo sideways and then to stop him. This is not a party trick but rather a test of how much discipline, attention and respect you have.

3-5 The sequence below shows Pelo working on stopping and turning at a distance. My left hand points towards his quarters, applying visual pressure. We both know I am too far away to back up my request with tactile pressure if he ignores me. However, his previous training is well established and he brings his head to me as his quarters turn away, and awaits the next visual cue.

6 It's not just horses that like to stay in the comfort zone – it's riders and handlers too! Keep thinking of new ways to challenge your horse (above). Provided it's within his physical and mental capabilities, he'll actually enjoy it. Following the stop and turn at a distance procedure, I direct Pelo towards a small log with a drop fence, over which he happily skips, despite me being yards away out of the frame.

Pressure can come from anywhere

At this point, let's just remind ourselves of where this is all going. As well as giving you some tools to add fun and variety to your horse's schooling, helping you gain his respect, focus and attention and improving physical dexterity and co-ordination in both of you, this work is all done with a view to improving your riding skills. The link between the two should by now become quite

obvious and, hopefully, you can see where and how it's going to start helping you both under saddle.

Of course, in your ridden work, due to the fact that you are only partially in your horse's field of vision as you sit on him, you are going to be using mainly tactile pressure rather than visual pressure, albeit as refined as you can possibly make it.

The point we must keep

returning to and confirming in the horse's mind is that he must give to pressure, no matter where it comes from or what format it takes. Whether it's the touch of a finger, a rope, a rein, a heel or a spur, he must respond by moving his shoulders, quarters, head, neck or whatever away from it.

LEADING LIGHTLY

Why always lead from a head collar? A horse that gives to pressure should lead from anything – a thread of cotton around his neck or a hand on his mane – or nothing at all (above).

REIN CONTACT

When you emulate rein contact in a groundwork session (above), the horse should move away.

RING THE CHANGES

Why always rope circle from a pressure halter? The horse should respond to the pressure round his neck on the same way (right). (For safety this rope is knotted in such a way that it cannot tighten round the horse's throat.)

LETTING GO AND BUILDING TRUST

'Letting go' and 'keeping your distance' is as much a mental as a physical discipline. Here Pelo is completely loose yet chooses to follow me over a fence.

Although he gets carried away with the excitement of jumping, Pelo's ear is still locked on to me and he continues to follow my lead even when his adrenalin is up.

Preparing for long lining

With any young horse or one that is new to you, it's essential to start at the beginning, even if you think you're stating the obvious. Horses can appear to be well schooled, then you discover that there are large gaps in the foundations, which crumble as the training becomes more advanced!

Groundwork establishes respect, develops understanding and improves your horse's physical and mental dexterity in preparation for riding. To help him make that connection between groundwork and ridden commands, he needs to learn to long line. He should now be responding readily to your commands and reading your body language when in hand and during rope circling, so it's not such a big step to add an outside rein and 'ride' him from the ground.

When preparing a youngster for backing, long lining is an absolutely vital piece of the jigsaw. The position of the lines means that directions come to the horse via his flanks – as when the rider applies a leg aid – and to his mouth – as when the rider applies a rein aid. The benefit is that the horse can learn to balance, carry and co-ordinate himself without the additional burden of a rider, but is 'listening backwards' and thinking about what is going on behind him. For an older horse that has become stale or unresponsive, long lining can be a new stimulus and different way of explaining things.

Long lining also helps you, the rider, to develop your own co-ordination, and see exactly how the horse is using himself.

Once again, before starting long lining, make sure the horse

> ### REMEMBER
>
> *Long lines should be about 3m (10ft) longer than the standard lunge rein, to allow enough length for the outside rein to come into play without restricting the horse.*

understands the basic principle of pressure and release. If he moves quickly and easily away from pressure (or better, the mere anticipation of pressure) on the ground, he will be well on the way to understanding more complex and subtle ridden aids at a later stage. You owe it to the horse, particularly a youngster, to spend the time teaching him from the ground to minimize the stress and discomfort of having a rider on board. You'll also make life much easier for yourself!

If you don't know whether your horse has long lined before, begin your first long lining session with the 'Introducing the long lines' exercise (pp.74–75) for safety's sake.

LONG LINING VERSUS LUNGEING

It's not that I am totally against lungeing, I just find rope circling and long lining more beneficial for all the reasons I've already stated, and lungeing can be dull in comparison. It's not very interactive and if the handler gets bored, there is a great chance that the horse will get bored, too.

I have an old horsemanship manual, which has a good few pages dedicated to the art of lungeing but only one paragraph on long lining. It acknowledges that a higher standard

of training can be achieved with long lining, but pretty much goes on to say that it is difficult to master so leave it to the experts! I totally agree that a higher level of training can be achieved, but I totally disagree that only experts should use it. Yes, it takes practice, but then doesn't anything that's worth doing? Learning to ride is not easy either, and if you've got the co-ordination for that then you can long rein.

This is probably a good place for one of my favourite phrases: 'It's not practice that makes perfect but perfect practice that makes perfect.' By that I don't mean you have to be perfect, but just know what it is you are trying to achieve and get help if necessary. I've always succeeded in teaching anyone to be perfectly competent at long lining within just a couple of days.

For me, another factor against lungeing is the amount of control you have when lungeing. How much do you have? That's for you to answer individually, of course, but all I can say is I've seen far too many horses tearing round for five minutes or more, doing entirely their own thing, with the handler standing on the middle, pleading for 'whoa' and not getting it! When the horse has had enough, he decides he'll stop, all on his own terms and completely in control of his own movement and direction. You don't really have any way of interrupting him apart from wheeling him in, which gives him a break from what he was supposed to be doing on the circle.

Now on the long lines, when you put a horse to work you have control over the inside rein and the outside rein, so in effect you are riding him from the ground. You can change direction without having to stop and can even progress to being able to do all your lateral work, figures of eight, flying changes, extensions down the long side, you name it – it just means you have to do a bit more running!

HOW MUCH LONG LINING DO I DO?

Unbacked youngster: no more than five times a week for a maximum of 10 minutes each time.

Older backed horse: no longer than 20 minutes and that is when they are fit. Do lots of changes of direction. When you start to get really good at it, try coming off the circle and using the long side of the school. You could also try some extensions, figures of eight and so on (it will get you fit at the same time). Do long lining to add variety to your schooling programme. I do something on the lines once a week.

Problem horse: with severe ridden problems I would go back to groundwork until I was achieving respect, a more forward way of going, engagement of the hindquarters and an overall much stronger horse. Do 15–20 minutes a day five times a week for up to five weeks. I know it sounds a real drag but it really is worth it.

Once your horse is going much better, keep long lining as part of your normal schooling programme, using it once a week. Long lining achieves quality schooling, therefore, it is demanding and tiring, so please watch your horses and remember to end the session before he does it for you!

CONTROLS FOR LONG LINING

I believe in making my life simple so when I am working a horse on lines I have only two verbal commands: a kissing or a clucking noise for upward transitions and 'whoa' for downward transitions. I am not saying don't talk to your horse, its just that I find it much easier to teach them two principles rather than a whole vocabulary. Think back to lungeing. How many people end up pleading with their horses? You can just imagine it: 'walk', 'waaalk', 'waaaaaalk', 'pleeease walk'. I have done it myself, and the horse carries on with his fingers in his ears, singing, 'I can't hear you'. Here are the steps:

▷ *To get a horse to go forward into a transition I flick the outside rein and cluck.*

▷ *Once the horse is going forward I stop clucking and flicking the line.*

▷ *As soon as he starts to slow down I repeat the previous two steps.*

▷ *When he is going in a nice steady rhythm I ask for the next pace in exactly the same way, thus teaching him that the clucking and the line being flicked simply mean 'go faster'.*

▷ *Eventually you won't need to flick the line, as the horse will go on the clucking noise.*

▷ *To slow down I say 'whoa' and take up a contact on the outside rein (as you would if you were riding), again the horse soon learns that 'whoa' means slow down.*

▷ *If he slows down too much, I cluck at him and flick the line. It doesn't take long for most horses to get the idea.*

CHANGING REIN

This is what panics people the most, but it just takes a bit of practice, honestly. Do it in walk until you have the hang of it. When I run courses, on the first day most of my clients moan, 'I'll never be able to do it', but by day three they look like professionals. Here's how it's done:

▷ *If you have your horse on the right rein, put both reins in your right hand. Run your left hand as far down the outside rein as you can and start to turn his head away from you. At the same time allow the inside line to run through your hand; this now becomes your new outside line.*

▷ *To do the turn smoothly you must have lines at least 10m (30ft) long: most lunge lines are 3m (10ft) too short.*

▷ *If you are struggling with the concept ask a friend to help you. Get him or her to stand with their back to you, put the middle of the line round the back of their neck and under their arms, send them out on a circle and practise turning them. It's great fun. I do it to people at the demos and it really does help.*

STEP-BY-STEP GUIDE TO LONG LINING

1 If your horse has never worked on long lines, introduce them slowly. Attach a rope to the halter or the bit ring. From the other side take it along the horse's back, to the quarters.

3&4 The rope circling work taught him to turn towards the pressure, that is towards the handler. Now he must learn to respond to pressure from the rope itself, which is telling him to turn the other way. Be patient, stand still, keep applying gentle pressure and he will work it out. It'll probably happen in bit of a rush the first time. Repeat the lesson until he calmly turns away from you towards the pressure, and even starts to anticipate the pressure and turn without being asked.

2 Repeat this on the other side. Drape it around the horse's back end if he is quite relaxed. He may find seeing you on one side, yet feeling pressure on the other disconcerting at first, but quietly persist until any natural panic reaction subsides. Stay on this opposite side and ask him to turn by putting pressure on the rope.

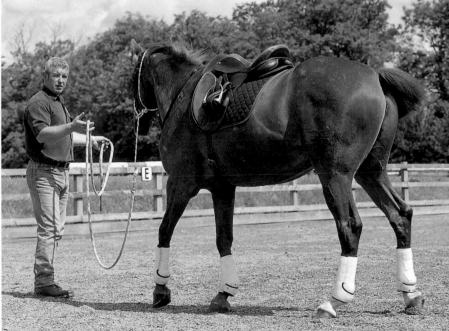

5 This is a big lesson – Troy has learnt that commands can come from apparently invisible sources, but that his response must remain the same and he must yield to pressure in order to make life comfortable again. This exercise is worth repeating many times, particularly to accustom the horse to the feeling of a rope around his hocks and back end. Don't be too precious about allowing the rope to drop low so he feels it against his legs. It is this lesson that will teach him not to panic when the lines inevitably go round his legs in the long reining process, or if you get in a muddle and need to drop them!

LONG LINING (continued)

Setting up the tack. Prepare for long lining by tacking up as usual, but secure the stirrups so they stay against his sides (a stirrup leather tying them under the belly is simple but effective). Make sure that the stirrups are not too long as you do not want them to bang his elbows. Either remove the reins or secure them in the throat lash before attaching a long line to each bit ring, above the reins if still attached (below).

Novice set up (right). This shows a rein set suitable for a novice horse or one new to long lining. The lines run from the bit through the stirrups to prevent them falling too low. This ensures that the outside rein comes behind the horse's quarters to encourage him to move forward and engage behind. The inside rein asks for flexion and direction, as in ridden work. As the horse works, the outside stirrup will create pressure to emulate that of the outside leg when riding, while the pressure from the inside stirrup comes off.

Intermediate set up (right and inset). A rein set suitable for an intermediate horse, with the rein contact coming a little higher due to a homemade clip and ring attached to the D-ring of the saddle. This set up encourages the horse to work in a more collected outline.

…set ups, from novice to advanced

Advanced set up. The most advanced position for the reins has the rein set over the withers again in a homemade loop from one D-ring to the other. This most closely emulates the position of the rider's hands while riding and asks for real opening and lift from the shoulders. You can see how the horse initially resists this request for more collection (below) then accepts it (bottom). With this rein position, you need to be careful to flip the reins over the cantle during a change of direction. This shouldn't alarm the horse at all if you've done your homework.

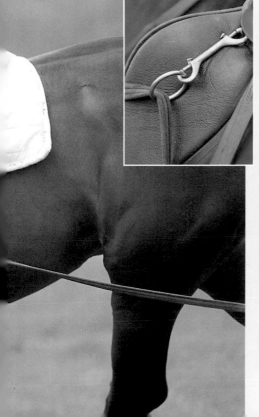

LONG LINING (continued)

Turning (right). 'Drop' the inside line and move towards the horse's back end as you shorten the outside line. Remember he needs to turn away from you, not towards you as he has been doing with the rope circling (see pp.74–75 and 'Controls for long lining', p.73). The slack from the old inside line will quickly be taken up as the horse turns. In the advanced set up, shown here, the reins need to be flicked over the cantle as the horse turns. For novice and intermediate set ups they follow the horse's side.

Change the rein (below). Practise all the manoeuvres – forwards, backwards and sideways and changing the rein – in walk at first. As you both become more co-ordinated, you should be able to ask him for upwards and downwards transitions from all paces. Don't demand perfection from the start. It will take you both a little while to get the feel of it. As with the first stage of the groundwork, you will have to exaggerate your commands initially but with improved understanding will come increasing subtlety (see also 'Controls for long lining', p.73).

…changing direction and pace

No **fuss (below and below right).** When they start long lining, many people have two main worries: one, that their horse will panic at the feeling of lunge lines on his sides, and two, that the lines will become tangled round the horse's legs. With the starter horse, it is vital that he is prepared for strange sensations, and this is best done now in a controlled environment! A horse that learns to accept pressure and the feeling of something unusual along his flanks and around his legs will be much safer and more relaxed to ride.

It's a good test of your horse's trust in you – if you have prepared properly during the first stage of the groundwork, he should simply stop if things go wrong and calmly wait while you sort them out. Don't attempt long lining if you think that he might panic; be sure that he won't panic by preparing him thoroughly.

Getting join-up without a round pen

I have often found out new and useful things by mistake or just by having the confidence to try something with a horse to see what happens. If it seems to work I'll try it again with another horse to see if the first time was just a fluke. This is one of the ways I learn and progress, continually developing my training system by using the horse as my teacher. You might find the same answer by asking a different question: that's what makes life exciting, and it's why one person's way is never the only way. As I said in my introduction, more than one road leads to Rome.

About three years ago, I did a series of demonstrations based around ground training; there were no round pens and I didn't do join-up. What I was trying to show was that training halters aren't magic bits of rope but a useful tool to help you in your goal. With most of the volunteer horses, the main problem was loading, and what I wanted to show was that you shouldn't just put a halter on him and take him to the lorry, but first spend time with him, do the groundwork and get his respect and trust. (It might seem like a long way around but in the end, it's time well invested.)

So I would do a little halter work with these horses, then I would long line them with lots of changes of direction to get them listening to me. I would wait until they were balanced and confident, before

asking them to approach the ramp of the lorry or trailer – one of the final stages in the loading process, not one of the first! The horses didn't always walk straight in, but it didn't take too long and I certainly didn't get the fight I used to get in the early days when my approach was more direct. I was beginning to learn that less was more.

My routine was to untack the horse at the end of the long lining session and go and talk to the audience, before I put the halter on and headed for the lorry. After a few demos I started to realize that during this chat with the audience, the horse was there at my shoulder – where ever I went he followed. I realized that I had achieved join-up simply from long lining, without ever using a round pen. Subsequent demos proved it happened time and time again, and not only that but it was a really strong join-up, not as tenuous as it can be when you have sent the horse away in a round pen in the traditional way.

This was a great discovery, as most of the people I help don't have round pens. It also got me thinking about the whole join-up process. I came to the conclusion that it is the fact that the herd leader has control over movement and direction that is important; it doesn't matter what form that control takes. When you are halter training and long lining, you, as the handler, are controlling the movement and direction, and the

more changes of direction you do, the more this is compounded.

I'll give you another example. When it's not the breeding season, I turn Pelo, my gelding, out with Nosey, my stallion, as they are great friends most of the time and I hate stallions to be segregated. Now I get on with both of these horses, but if I go in the field to see Pelo, Nosey will not let me near him. He will keep himself between me and Pelo, and keep moving Pelo off in different directions. Pelo is usually a very dominant horse but he sees Nosey as the boss and doesn't even question him. That's exactly what you are doing when long lining. You don't need a round pen. Especially with a horse that you've had for ages or an older horse that you want to join-up with, long lining and halter training, using as many changes of pace and direction as you can, might be the solution you are looking for.

Checking your progress

Can you answer 'yes' to *all* of the following? If not work out where you are going wrong and go back to that section of the book to learn more.

▷ Am I always completely clear and consistent in my commands, however tired and frustrated I may be?

▷ Do I calmly insist on the horse doing the right thing, however long it takes, then immediately reward him for it?

▷ Is it completely clear to the horse when he is right and when he is wrong?

▷ Do I reward the horse with my approval and a removal of the pressure? This is enough: leave bribes, titbits, threats and compromise out of it.

▷ Am I picking up subtle changes in behaviour, attitude and body language and acknowledging their significance?

▷ Is my horse self-motivated and eager to please during the sessions? If he's carrying out his duties reluctantly and with the minimum of effort, have I examined the reasons why?

▷ Am I being fair in what I ask for? Horses are usually more than generous once they understand what is expected, but unfair requests can cause them to become sour and frustrated. Remember that 20 minutes of long lining is roughly equivalent to an hour's hack, so start gently and build up.

▷ Am I asking enough? Once you've laid the foundations, your horse's education must be progressive. As well as preventing boredom, your aim is to progress to an ever more subtle form of communication and higher skill level.

▷ Am I well disciplined myself? An 'it'll do for today…' attitude won't clarify things for the horse.

▷ Do I treat each obstacle as an opportunity to learn and develop my relationship with my horse, rather than a setback?

▷ Are my signals polite requests to the horse to do what I want him to do, not demands?

Key lessons to take forward

Your work so far should have:

▷ Given you some tools to add more find and variety to your horse's schooling.

▷ Helped you gain his respect, focus and attention.

▷ Improved physical dexterity and co-ordination in both of you..

▷ Encouraged him to discover means to self-carriage.

▷ Given you the means to take control of movement and direction without necessarily riding.

3 Making the connection to ridden work

What you should know before you start

The work in this chapter is intended both for ridden horses and novices that have never had a rider. If your horse is experienced, you can turn to p.92 to begin learning how to transfer what you have done so far into ridden exercises, although there are some useful ideas in this section. If your horse is a starter, please read the next few pages, before continuing.

STARTING A YOUNGSTER

Starting a horse can be an exciting journey, and it's easy to lose sight of the fact that riding the animal comes a long way down the road leading to true horsemanship, not at the beginning! In my opinion, the main object in training a horse is to teach him that wherever he finds pressure and discomfort (not necessarily from the handler, it could be in any situation), be it physical, emotional or mental, the person handling him represents comfort and security.

Don't make any demands of your horse under saddle until you have a willing, obedient and balanced animal from the ground; if he can't carry his own weight with comfort and balance, he's unlikely to be able to carry yours. By obedient, I don't mean 'robotic'! I like a horse to retain its character and expression, while remaining safe and under control.

If you have laid a firm foundation of knowledge, understanding and trust, then the moment you first saddle up or sit astride your horse shouldn't be the big deal it is sometimes hyped up to be. With careful and sympathetic preparation from the ground, there is no reason why your horse shouldn't calmly accept all you ask of him and willingly submit to being ridden.

ALLOW MISTAKES

To my mind, the biggest drawback with many so-called 'traditional' methods is that the horse is not allowed to make mistakes – it's almost as if the handler is frightened of the possible consequences. For example, when putting a saddle on a horse for the first time, there is very often someone at his head to stop him reacting. I think this attitude inhibits the horse's learning. While it is important to keep things safe so that no-one gets hurt and the horse isn't frightened, this shouldn't be an issue if you've done your groundwork

and the horse has confidence in you. So my way of introducing the saddle is to make sure I am in a safe environment, clip a long lead rope (8m/25ft) on to a head collar if necessary, put the saddle on and then let the horse 'express' himself with it – for some horses this might involve plenty of bucking or cantering around the menage, others might walk a bit strangely for a few paces and then accept it happily. Let him learn that it won't harm him. I think this is an important experience for a horse; he learns that he can come through it and be OK. You don't overcome fears, or get accustomed to things which give you an adrenalin buzz, without actually doing them.

One of the first horses I had in my yard was a 10-year-old eventer that had started not wanting to go forward. As was normal for me under these circumstances at the time, I put him in the round pen, got him joined-up then put the tack on, and let him loose. Despite his age and the fact that he was an experienced eventer, he was off, bucking and kicking like a youngster with his first saddle. The truth was that although

COMFORT ZONE

When you successfully school your horse using my methods, he will be happy for you to take the lead and will see you as a safe haven.

he was co-operating as best he could with the process of being ridden, this horse had never truly accepted the saddle. On its own this did not cure the napping problem but it showed me that horses can be very giving. This chap did his job even though there was that huge doubt in the back of his mind.

A horse that has not been *properly* prepared is quite within his rights to flee physically, and/or shut down mentally and emotionally. Newly backed youngsters performing rodeo spectacles make exciting viewing but in most cases, they reveal a breakdown of trust and communication between horse and handler, which is exactly what we don't want. This is not letting the horse explore the saddle in a controlled environment, but eliciting a total right-brain reaction (see p.37) where he truly feels that he is fighting for his life. While it's only right to give due respect to the fact that his natural instincts may cause the horse to react in an unpredictable way, whatever his age, if you have done your work thoroughly then really it should be just 'another day at the office' as far as he is concerned.

Things go wrong because convincing an animal with the size and strength of a horse to work willingly and co-operatively with you demands a number of skills, and experience or talent are not necessarily among them – patience, common sense and empathy can get you where you need to go. However, there is one proviso: if you are backing a horse for the first time, I strongly recommend that you have some experienced help. It's a most crucial time and a simple mistake can be disastrous.

HAVE YOU GOT WHAT IT TAKES?

You need experience, patience and intuition to start a horse successfully. Make sure your ego is not going to get in the way.

Ask yourself:

▷ *What do I hope to get out of the experience? The question may sound obvious, but the answer often isn't! Perhaps you dream of producing a better-trained horse than you could buy, or maybe you've bred the animal and have a natural interest in taking the next step. Whatever your reason for doing it, make sure it's not just ego!*

▷ *Are my aims compatible with the horse's ability? Rosettes mean nothing to him, and being too fixed on long-term performance goals may prevent you being as intuitive as you need to be when interpreting daily feed-back from your horse.*

▷ *Can I keep the words 'should' or 'must' out of my think-ing and dialogue whenever my horse is concerned? The true path to success is to present everything in a way that the horse can understand, which means logically and in accordance with his physiological make up.*

▷ *Am I prepared to ask for advice and direction? Furthermore, will I try to interpret and use it with sensi-tivity? Forget the favourite guru of the moment. Find a coherent theory that makes sense to you and works for your horse.*

▷ *Do I believe in myself? While respecting the enormity of what you are trying to do, you also need to keep it in perspective and have faith in your own ability. You are going to have fun and learn together and out of your mutual understanding will come performance, but it is not the main object: it's a side effect.*

▷ *Can I learn patience, if only for the duration I am han-dling my horse? Remember that when you watch videos or attend demonstrations which involve young horses, the people concerned are usually extremely experienced and have a different aim to yours. You don't have to do things exactly as they do, or as quickly. Being able to start a horse in a very short period of time is not neces-sarily an indication of greatness.*

IS YOUR HORSE READY?

Be sure that your horse trusts you and is relaxed, confident and obedient in his groundwork and distance work, before you start introducing him to ridden work.

Ask yourself:

▷ *Does he understand absolutely the concept of pressure and release (see pp.46–53)? He should be confident, obedient and competent in both his groundwork and his distance training.*

▷ *Can I see daily signs of his trust and confidence in me? For example, when approaching him in the paddock, does he prick up his ears and make eye contact or look away and try to find an escape route?*

▷ *At gates or door, does he stop at a respectful distance back and wait politely for me to open it, or does he creep into my personal space and barge me out of the way?*

▷ *While being groomed and handled, does he stand quietly and appear to enjoy the attention?*

▷ *When I introduce tack or other equipment, does he regard it with calm curiosity, with not a hint of fear or suspicion, even when I touch him with it?*

MORE PRESSURE AND RELEASE WORK

Here I am teaching Scarlet the need to move towards pressure when it comes from above her. At first she resists then, as a result of her training from the ground and correct halter training from an early age, she gives in and gets herself organized. While this is a good lesson for any horse, I believe this is excellent preparation for backing. By the age of three, Scarlet is a calm and co-operative young horse. She is used to seeing riders looming above her and generally enjoys the attention, rather than being threatened by the sight of me up there!

Before mounting. Be absolutely sure your foundations are solid so that the connection between groundwork and ridden work is an obvious one for your horse. Yes, it's back to that all-important understanding of pressure and release!

…learning how to give to pressure from above

Teaching the aids

So your horse has been well prepared, and shown himself willing to make the ultimate concession for a prey animal – that is, to allow you on his back. However old he is and however often you ride, take a little time to respect and appreciate the enormity of this submission every time you swing your leg over his back: thousands of years of evolution have developed his instincts to react against it, yet there he stands, awaiting your instructions.

> Good riding is really just about asking the right question at the right time in the right way, and rewarding the right answer. The principles remain the same, no matter what level you are at.

The least we can do as riders is develop the skills we need to make it as pleasant an experience as possible for the horse, so that we help or 'aid' him, rather than hinder. It's not as easy as it sounds, of course, and it is a learning process that lasts a lifetime! But it's important not to be intimidated by the prospect. After all, good riding is really just about asking the right question at the right time in the right way, and rewarding the right answer. The principles remain the same, no matter what level you are at.

Every horse can perform so-called 'advanced' movements such as piaffe, pirouette and flying changes, because they are natural movements, learnt and used extensively in the wild for defence, play and mating. What we strive for as riders is the ability to produce them on demand. We do this using pressure in a variety of places and combinations to create what we call aids. Aids are the means by which the rider guides the horse through his working exercises. Schooling is the process of teaching a horse what each of the aids mean, so he can link the signal with the movement required.

The horse should already have been taught to yield to pressure in his groundwork, so it's the next logical step for him to make the connection between this and the pressure he feels from your hands, legs or seat when you're riding. Now you can see why a total understanding of pressure and release forms the basis of your training programme, and is the key to successful schooling.

THE BASIC AIDING SYSTEM

While on a highly schooled animal the results achieved through using the aids look spectacular, the means by which they are communicated to

PRINCIPLES OF CONTACT

What is your horse's reaction to rein contact? Pinning a horse's head down just doesn't work, and this exercise will show you why.

With your arm stretched straight out in front of you to represent the horse's neck, use the other hand to try and force it down, always resisting with the other arm. Any success? Where is the tightness in your muscles? And what happens when you remove the force? The 'neck' springs up even higher!

Now, try the opposite – push your arm up from beneath, as if you were trying to encourage the 'neck' to go even higher, again use resistance. You should feel the muscles working along the top of your outstretched arm rather than below, and when you remove the opposing force, the natural response in your muscles makes your arm lower.

Everyone, from weekend rider to Grand Prix competitor, has the same basic tools to work with: legs, seat and hands.

the horse is actually quite simple. Everyone, from weekend rider to Grand Prix competitor, has the same basic tools to work with: legs, seat and hands. You just get different results depending on how these basic ingredients are blended.

▷ Use LEG for impulsion, changes of pace, bending and displacing the horse: in effect for control of the haunches.

▷ Use SEAT when you are ready to refine the leg aids, to aid bending and to communicate more directly with the horse's back to ask for longer or shorter steps.

▷ Use HAND to receive the energy created by the leg, to give the horse a limit within which he must work his frame and to aid the direction of the forehand and bending.

You only have to be able to do two things with your aids: 'ask' and 'correct', but to do these well you need a good seat.

A well-schooled horse has a good understanding of a wide range of aid combinations and responds to them immediately. This allows the rider to control the horse's speed, rhythm, forward movement, bend through the body and length of stride. A well-schooled rider not only has a good understanding of a wide range of aid combinations, but also has control of his own hands, legs, seat and body so he can apply them correctly to control and communicate with the horse!

You only have to be able to do two things with your aids: 'ask' and

COMPATIBILITY

If you are struggling to maintain a correct position, remember that there are two of you playing this game! The horse has his own preferences and will try to 'dislodge' you accordingly.

A horse's back moves in three planes – horizontal (backwards and forwards), vertical (up and down) and lateral (side-to-side). What you are aiming for is to follow the horse's movement through these three planes, but also for him to 'aid' you in doing that. You need to ask him to move in a way that is compatible with your seat, rather than stay with his movement until you reach a compromise. He will have a way of going that he finds most comfortable, and will try to 'disengage' your seat to be compatible with it. A good example of this is the one-sided horse that tries to make life easier for itself by throwing you onto a particular trot diagonal, or always taking the same canter lead. Because it's usually much more comfortable for the rider too, you may not be inclined to insist on the correct option. In fact, you may not even be aware of what the horse is doing. The stronger your seat, the better you can cope with the 'assault' from the horse.

If you have a horse that throws you to one side or prefers one lead over the other, go back to the long lines, watch how he moves, identify the inconsistencies and start to correct them (see also p.140).

'correct', but to do these well you need a good seat (see Cavalry Capers, p.94).

LEARNING TO SIT WELL

The seat is the 'control headquarters' or platform from which all other aids initiate. With an independent seat you'll be able to balance over the horse's centre of gravity at all three paces without gripping, and harmonize with the horse at all paces, thereby 'staying out of his way' and allowing him to develop these paces without disturbance. Without an independent seat, you can't confirm to the horse what's right and what's wrong. It's not so much a matter of giving the right aids as not giving aids when you don't mean to! Remember, a horse just responds to different pressures as and when requested. He won't ask himself if you really meant what he felt!

Learning to sit well is one of the hardest things for any rider, and it can take years to develop, so don't expect instant results! An instructor can shout at you to 'sit deep' or 'keep a line through ear to shoulder, hip and heel', but you won't be able to maintain this until your confidence, balance, co-ordination and feel have developed sufficiently to allow it to happen. Those lucky riders who appear to be 'naturals' don't necessarily have some magic power or god-given empathy. What they probably do have are certain biomechanical advantages that make it easier for them to maintain the correct position, such as long lean legs that can wrap closely around the horse, and inherent characteristics such as good balance and co-ordination. But you can develop a good seat if you put yourself in the right situation.

CAVALRY CAPERS

When I was instructing recruits in the Household Cavalry, a high percentage of them had never even been up close to a horse let alone ridden one, and we had only 20 weeks to turn them into riders who could carry out ceremonial duties, which for the main part are done at sitting trot. Once a week, on a Saturday, we did what we called a 'blanket ride' when the recruits rode on a blanket folded up and kept in place by a surcingle.

For the first few weeks the recruits spent most of their time on the floor, and I spent most of my time laughing. Those old cavalry horses were full of humour and you could almost see the glint in their eye on Saturday mornings, as the recruits came round the corner. But as the weeks progressed, those recruits developed Velcro seats, and the biggest improvement in their riding came between the Saturday ride and Monday morning. They had to learn to become balanced, co-ordinated and have a deeper seat so that they didn't fall off. If you have a sensible horse and a safe environment, why not try some blanket riding? Obviously you need to be safe so don't do it on a youngster or a difficult horse. The aim is to improve, not fall off. Another option would be to go and have some lessons on the lunge at a reputable establishment.

DEVELOPING SUBTLETY

Why shout when you can whisper? To achieve subtlety of response from the horse, you must be subtle in your commands. Even if you are pretty sure he won't respond to a light touch of your leg, you must never give up the possibility that he might. Steam in with brutal aids and you'll simply deaden him to the possibility of more subtle communication, and reduce the chance of harmonious co-operation. It's no good telling yourself that 'he started it' – you have superior reasoning power, so it's up to you to finish it.

Before you can become subtle you have to have a forward and responsive horse. There is no point in even trying to be subtle if your horse isn't listening to you. While our aim is to be as refined as possible, there are times when you have to be very obvious in your actions until your horse learns what you mean. Once your horse is responding to the very

obvious then you can start to become more subtle.

DEAD TO THE LEG?

Think of that old riding school pony with a child banging up and down on it, kick, kick, kick, every day. Does the pony go any faster? Never. Yet that very same pony in the field will shudder as a fly lands on his skin. There's nothing wrong with his nerve endings except they have shut down to the stimulus of a child banging away with its heels. In this situation, what we need to do is change the stimulus so that the mind is reactivated.

With the problem of a horse not wanting to go forward from the leg, I would use a 'wip-wop' or 'over and under' (see opposite). A wip-wop is different from a whip because it isn't one-sided, it flicks over the withers and behind the leg from one side to the other. Think of the cowboys riding out of town in the old western

movies, with their long reins moving from side to side across the horse's withers. This isn't done to look good but to create forward movement – the action of the rein going across the withers and back again creates a form of psychological pressure.

To make the action of the wip-wop effective, it needs to back up the usual aid and it must stop moving as soon as the horse goes forward. So, for example, in halt use your legs to ask your horse to move forward (using as much leg as you ultimately want to use – very little); if he doesn't respond, give him a flick with the wip-wop rather than using more leg. As soon as you get a response stop using it. Some horses will respond very quickly and you will have to do this only a few times before they will start to move at the first ask, others take a little longer. You will get to a stage where if, for example, you are in working trot and your horse starts to slow down, lifting the arm that carries the wip-wop will cause your horse to pick up the pace. This is how you get subtlety.

REFINING THE AIDS

When schooling, every time you apply an aid, you've got to monitor the horse's response to ensure that you're using as little pressure as possible while still being effective. By doing this you can refine the aids and communicate with the horse in an increasingly subtle way, which is more pleasant for you both. A well-schooled horse is not responding to the pressure of aids so much as the cues that he has learnt precede them – that's why a clever rider can make it look like he isn't doing anything except sit there!

SUCCESS WITH A WIP-WOP

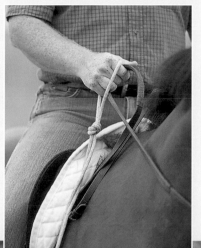

Find an old lead rope, cut off the clip, fold the rope in half and tie a knot at the end to form a loop (left). Put this on your wrist so it is just hanging there until you want to use it (unlike with a conventional whip, it is safe to do this with a wip-wop).

Introduce your horse to the wip-wop in a safe environment, such as a manege, indoor school or a small fenced paddock. When you first try this, even the quietest horse will often shoot forward – be prepared and have a loose but safe length of rein so that you do not smack your horse in the mouth. If you are worried, you could always use a neck strap as well for added security.

If you are finding the movement difficult, practise at home sitting on a chair. Hold the wip-wop in your hand while still on your wrist, but don't try using it like a whip, it just won't work. Move it over the withers and behind the leg in an arc, backwards and forwards, or from side-to-side. Keep thinking of those cowboys!

ARE YOU DELEGATING?

You will hamper your progress if you do not give the horse the chance to exercise his own decision-making powers. Can you be sure you are doing none of the following?

▷ *Constantly 'nagging' with your aids so the horse never gets the chance to exercise his own initiative.*

▷ *Refusing to delegate responsibility for the basics, such as rhythm, energy, outline and direction, ie over-riding.*

▷ *Feeling you can't delegate, usually because you have a sneaky suspicion that the foundations are not as solid as they should be.*

▷ *Thinking you are delegating, when in fact you're not!*

to make their own decisions, even if they have a secret fear that the child will make mistakes or do something wrong, otherwise they will be dependent all their lives. Likewise, there comes a time when you should be delegating more and more responsibility to the horse (see left). As he becomes more advanced in his training, it becomes his job to maintain the basics such as rhythm, energy, outline and the path you have set him on, so you can concentrate on refining the next stage. It's like a composer, who must first of all write down the basic tune on paper and get

Think about someone asking you to do something. How do you prefer them to do it? This should give you a good idea of how you should communicate with your horse. If someone walked up to you and shouted, 'Get me a cup of tea this instant', your attitude towards them (and your willingness to get their tea) would be very negative. If they got tea at all, it would probably be with a bad grace on your part. And, of course, as soon as you start making the tea, you'd expect the nagging to stop. When you gave it to the person concerned, you'd expect thanks, even if you hadn't made it exactly the way they normally have it. If they're nice about it, you probably wouldn't mind them mentioning that they prefer a little more sugar. When you really get to like them, you'll spot the signs that they're ready for a cuppa, and already have the kettle on and their favourite mug out before they ask.

HANDING OVER RESPONSIBILITY

As children get older, parents have to step back and give them the freedom

the musicians familiar with it, before he can ask for greater expression here or different timing there. With horses, you cannot add artistry without a solid framework in place.

To develop a self-motivated and independent-minded horse, you need to play fair and start to give your horse the opportunity to show that he is working things out for himself. By doing correct ground training you are giving your horse the tools to enable him to be responsible for himself. Take, for example, the horse that doesn't like to go forward; once you have got him responding to the

wip-wop, it would be unfair to constantly start your requests with it. It's fairer to ask with your leg first to give him the chance to do the right thing, only if he doesn't comply should you correct him using the wip-wop. If you don't allow your horse to make a mistake he will never learn. And once he's got the hang of it, let him do it: there's nothing worse than someone asking you to take responsibility for a task for which you have been preparing for months, then hanging over your shoulder saying, 'Oh no, not like that!' all the time.

> If you don't allow your horse to make a mistake he will never learn. And once he's got the hang of it, let him do it...

TIMING

This is another crucial part of developing refinement and subtlety, not to mention retaining your horse's good will and co-operation. No matter how confusing or frustrating you find it all, a logical and fair training system always follows the pattern of pressure, response, release.

When the horse responds correctly to your aids, he must be rewarded by the pressure releasing immediately, which confirms to him that his response was correct.

Cues are conditioned responses. Problems arise when you stop supporting the cue with a reward, and the learning curve breaks down. Basically, it seems to the horse that you're not keeping your half of the bargain, and he's right. This doesn't mean you have to stop what you're doing and feed him carrots every time he does as he's asked: just as you refine your aids down to a subtle cue, you can refine your rewards to a murmur of your voice or a softening of the hand on the rein for example. Every time you ask something of your horse, ask the question he will be asking – what's in it for me? The answer is that it is either a removal of a negative factor (for example, release of pressure) or the addition of a positive factor (for example, a pat or verbal praise). Both negative and positive reinforcement are effective means of developing your horse's understanding of cues. Neither includes 'punishment', which is not an effective way to train a horse.

WHO'S RESPONSIBLE?

From past experience Troy thinks that there's no point in responding to increased pressure. He needs careful groundwork to be reassured that if he responds to a request he will be rewarded instantly.

WORKING ON CONTACT

Hands up exercise. An automatic reaction when the horse's head comes up is for the rider's hands to come down. In fact, it makes more sense to raise your hands to follow the movement of the horse's head. Re-read 'Principles of contact', p.92.

1 Imagine you have a greasy pole coming out of each knee and going straight up in front of you, imagine sliding your hands up the greasy pole (so it's an upward pressure not a backward one). Keep a constant pressure and when you feel her taking the bit down release the pressure. You are trying to show her that the most comfortable place is with her head and neck in correct carriage, so every time she brings her head up, repeat the process. Eventually your raised hands will become modified to just a squeeze of the reins. This also prevents her building up opposing muscle groups in the neck.

2 Do this work at halt until your horse's reaction becomes automatic: you raise your hands; she lowers her head. This training supplements the groundwork that established a clear understanding of pressure and release in this mare's mind. (You can see her on pp.64–65 going through this process.) Remember, what impresses the horse most is not how quickly you put the pressure on but how quickly you remove it. Even if he only drops his a head a few inches, you must release the pressure. That is his reward, and for this training to work, you have to show the horse that there is something in it for him.

…how you improve your horse's response to the bit

This is another check to see that your horse responds to pressure and isn't resistant to the bit. It is also a fantastic exercise for him, opening up his vertebrae before he starts work.

Neck stretch. Apply enough pressure to bring his head as far round towards you as is comfortable for him. Use upward, not backward pressure. Initially your horse will probably think you are asking him to turn a circle, so make sure you are not using your leg and confusing him. Keep a consistent and constant pressure on the rein until he stops moving, then rub his face and release the pressure. Ask again until he turns his head to your knee without walking off – again, once he gives you his head, rub his face and release. Remember, at the beginning he may only be able to come part of the way until he supples up – always reward the smallest try. (To learn how to cope with resistance to the bit, see pp.142–143.)

Repeat. Take any opportunity to reinforce the message that wherever the pressure comes from or whatever form it takes, your horse should give to or move away from it.

Effective schooling

Like any form of education, it is important to stick to a planned curriculum so you (or future riders) will have a firm foundation on which to build. By following a logical path of progression, it doesn't really matter if you get a little sidetracked or have a set back – that's part of life with horses and your aims should still be clear. For most of us, the aims are for greater communication, collection and obedience, because that's the type of horse that makes a safe and pleasant ride, whether or not you're interested in competing.

Your curriculum will include exercises designed to develop the horse's physical abilities and mental understanding. Correctly ridden, their purpose is to encourage the horse to maintain a biomechanically correct outline (see p.58), so they are both an aid and a test for the horse. Think about it – you test for a particular skill by doing something that requires it, and that's why we use schooling exercises. As well as testing the extent of the horse's knowledge, so you know your questions are fair and appropriate, practising school movements and asking for more and more precision eventually improves the horse's mental and physical ability to carry out the task.

WHICH EXERCISES?

Equestrianism is full of fancy terms that are confusing to the uninitiated, but the fact is, horses don't care what you call a particular exercise, as long as it's logical and the aids are applied in a way he can understand.

All school exercises are made up of circles, lines and loops, designed to test the rider's control, co-ordination and accuracy with the aids, and the horse's obedience, understanding and physical ability. Whichever exercises you use, the important thing is to do them correctly, and the more variety you include, the better. Your aim is to develop your control of the horse's forward and sideways movement, such as transitions and lateral work. You want the horse to carry himself correctly and deliberately forwards or sideways in balanced way, not just fall there. At first, it's all about learning the steps and movements slowly. As you and your horse develop confidence and co-ordination, you can speed things up and put more into it, and it becomes much more fun and has far greater fitness benefits.

TRANSITIONS AND SELF-CARRIAGE

The schooling exercises that most improve self-carriage are probably transitions, because it's at the moment of transition that the horse

CHECKLIST OF FORWARDS AND SIDEWAYS CONTROL

▷ *Self-carriage – the horse should not be hollow (above the bit), overflex (behind the bit) or lean on the hand.*

▷ *Straightness – the horse should be tracking straight, the hind hoof prints following the line of the front prints. Is he tilting through his head or neck?*

▷ *When you offer your hand forward, the horse should lengthen his stride without running or being inactive.*

A SCHOOLING PROGRAMME

Include the exercises below in your schooling programme, but don't use all of them in every session.

▷ *Transitions – direct and progressive*

▷ *Spirals and small circles*

▷ *Straight lines*

▷ *Shorten and lengthen stride*

▷ *Changes of rein*

▷ *Lateral work*

Apart from your 10 minute warm up and 10 minute cool down, I recommend that you do no more than 20 minutes schooling a day. Choose something that you want to work on each time and limit yourself to that. Remember it's not 'practice makes perfect' but 'perfect practice that makes perfect', so enlist help if you aren't sure (even top riders have instructors). Vary where you do your schooling. Horses soon get bored of the arena, so if possible find somewhere on a hack or in a field where you can do some work. Once a month try devising your own dressage test, incorporating all that you have been working on, it only has to be 10 minutes long.

has to make the most gymnastic effort to use his body correctly. It's a common mistake for the rider to be relieved at having got the transition out of the way and so stay in the same pace for circuit after circuit. This is not helping the horse, and may well be an example of bad practice making matters worse, rather than perfect practice making perfect!

The value of transitions

▷ They call the horse's attention to the aids to make him alert and responsive.
▷ They test the rider's co-ordination and communication skills.
▷ The physical demand of changing pace induces the horse to increase engagement of the back and haunch muscles to bring the hind legs under more as they assume more of the weight carrying (collection), thereby lowering the haunches and raising the forehand.

These effects only occur if the style of the transition is correct.

Upward transitions

A horse can move from one pace up to the next one in three ways:

▷ by lifting and propelling himself with his hind leg in a state of balance;
▷ by falling forward through a loss of balance, onto the shoulder;
▷ by pulling himself forward from the forehand.

Only the first one, where the horse lifts himself with the hind leg in a state of balance with a constant outline in self-carriage, is correct.

Downward transitions

A horse can change pace downwards in one of three ways:

▷ by retaining his balance and progressively taking more weight back to the haunches;
▷ by falling forward onto the shoulder;
▷ by abruptly stopping his impulsion.

Only the first one, where the horse retains his balance on the haunches and maintains a constant outline in self-carriage, is correct.

Transitions within the pace

These are longitudinal exercises that aim to control the horse's ability to shift his centre of gravity towards the haunches and improve his ability to magnify his gaits in the direction of maximum length or maximum height.

WHAT IS A CLOSED REIN?

In its most obvious state, a closed rein is of even and consistent pressure and used to contain and control direction. If you want to move your horse to the left, close your right rein on to his neck, but not across his wither (remember you have taught him to move away from pressure where ever it comes from), and open the left rein away from his neck, again making it all very obvious. Once your horse understands, you can start to refine the aids down to a squeeze of the rein. (See 'The corridor of aids', pp.102–103, for more information.) Although this horse is responding nicely to his rider's request, he is slightly heavy in the hand.

THE CORRIDOR
OF AIDS

You'll make life easier for yourself and your horse if you use horse-logical aids – those that capitalize on what is natural or instinctive for a horse. For a flight animal, that means heading for the nearest opening – not literally an open door, but wherever he feels he can move away from the pressure of your aid.

Imagine viewing the horse's body from above as a corridor, with each limb being beside a door opening off it – the doors being your legs, seat and hands. When you ask for movement, you need to create an 'open door' in the corridor for the horse to slip through. That's why it's important to allow forward movement with the hands when you use your leg.

Moving the quarters (left). If you want the hindquarters to step to the right, you first need to open the door holding them in the corridor (your right leg) and speak nicely to the left hind (with your left leg) to ask it to step through. The hands and reins stay closed to keep the shoulders in the corridor.

Moving the shoulders (above). To move the right shoulder, first open the corresponding door (your right hand) and ask the left shoulder to move through. Remember, always open the door first to allow the movement you're asking for, otherwise you are asking your horse to bang his head against a brick wall!

SIDEWAYS MOVEMENT

If you have worked patiently and consistently through the groundwork exercises, you should have achieved a high level of obedience and competence in your lateral work already. This will make everything fall into place far more easily for both of you under saddle.

Lateral work is really important because it puts your co-ordination and understanding of aiding under the spotlight. It also tests the horse's understanding and response to your aids, improves his balance, develops strength and suppleness, which in turn will enhance his freedom of movement. As it works both sides of the horse independently and equally, it minimizes the chance of one-sidedness or crookedness developing and it will help link this creature of two halves into a whole. Most important of all, it increases your ability to control the horse. Lateral work boils down to control of the shoulders. Not just a useful party trick, for those interested in competition, control of the shoulders is the key to many ridden problems, including napping, spooking and running out at fences: 80 per cent of evasions come through the shoulder.

GETTING CONTROL OF THE SHOULDERS

I teach a horse that I can control the movement and direction of his shoulders through circling work. Straightness in a ridden horse will only be achieved if the rider has the ability to put the shoulders in front of the quarters, by learning to do this you can reduce enormously the likelihood of evasions (see also pp.140–141).

Controlling the shoulders when riding involves opening and closing the rein (see p.101). If your horse falls in through his right shoulder, for example, close the right rein by bringing your elbow into your waist and putting the rein against his neck, then open the left rein by moving your arm away from your side. This takes his nose to the left, away from the direction he is falling in, and his shoulders have to follow his nose, which puts them back in front of his quarters, that is, straight! Once he is going straight, leave him alone until he falls in through his shoulder again. If he does, repeat the process. You will find that the length of time between each correction will get longer. Resist the temptation to hold him straight all the time. Allow him to make the mistake then correct him. By training your horse in this way he will become self-motivated and take responsibility for keeping himself straight, leaving you free to concentrate on other things.

A CREATURE OF TWO HALVES

The fact that a horse prefers one direction over the other is something we learn early in our riding, and it isn't particularly surprising. Think about humans: no matter how hard a right-hander practises writing with the left hand, it's never quite the same. Research shows that horses have laterality or 'handedness' at least to the same degree as humans. For example, on a straight track and without any training, at least two out of every three will choose left lead canter or gallop over right lead. Most of us have experienced this ourselves when riding an untrained horse: it will prefer a particular rein, canter lead or trot diagonal. Laterality is well understood and acknowledged in Thoroughbred racing, since the success of a horse may depend on whether the racetrack is a left- or right-handed course. On an anti-clockwise racecourse where a horse would naturally choose left lead gallop, a clever jockey may ask for a change to the right lead on the final straight to bring into play relatively fresh muscle groups. Even at rest or when grazing, a horse, regardless of age, will often be seen to position one forelimb in front of the other. This is almost always the forelimb of the dominant diagonal pair, and more often than not it will be the left fore, which indicates right rear/left fore dominance, stemming from right sidedness.

But, as already outlined (pp.37–39), it's not just the horse's body that 'takes sides' – it's his brain. This training system develops left-brain thinking and by getting him to use the left side of his brain you are causing him to think, resulting in an

endorphic release, which calms and cancels out his instinctive adrenalin rush. Pressure halters work in a similar way, becoming a sort of 'comfort blanket'. When a horse has got one on and understands the system of pressure and release, he knows how to react, so any decision-making is out of his hands. It's a bit like going into an exam well prepared. Because you've done your homework and revision, on turning over that exam paper your nerves immediately subside because you see a row of questions you understand and know you can answer. When I

LATERALITY

Just as humans are right-handed or left-handed, so horses prefer one lead or diagonal. Even when grazing or at rest, a horse will favour one foreleg over the other.

was training racehorses to go into the starting stalls, some of them would only have to feel the halter to be relieved. They would start to yawn, mentally and emotionally comfortable in the knowledge that they understood what lay ahead.

Developing feel

'Feel', the 'Holy Grail' of equitation! Knowing exactly how much of each aid is needed to produce a particular result with an individual horse is called 'feel', the finishing touch that defines a gifted rider. Some riders have more natural 'feel' than others, but everyone can develop it – I believe that it comes with good timing, along with a combination of experience and empathy.

Consider the chef who can produce a wonderful meal without looking at a recipe book or measuring out precise ingredients. In the past, he will almost certainly have spent many hours practising how to make fine sauces by the book until he knows exactly how they should look, feel and taste, and each stage of the cooking process. He'll also have had his fair share of awful moments, when smoke poured out of the oven door and there were hungry guests waiting expectantly in the next room, and through this he will have learnt to spot the signs that all is not well at a much earlier stage and rescue the situation before it becomes serious. He probably also started with a love of good food, a knowledge of what he was aiming for and a desire to produce it for the pleasure of himself and others, with the minimum of mishaps in the kitchen.

This should be our aim when we're schooling our horses. You may never become a celebrity chef, but it's within everyone's power to produce good, wholesome fare that is a pleasure to partake. What we want is not a horse that can be described as 'on the bit', but one whose whole body is 'on the aids'.

The aim is to have a horse that is not only 'on the bit', but also on all the rest of the aids, too.

Common aiding problems

If the results you get aren't quite those you'd hoped for, one of the following is usually at the root:

▷ You are applying too much pressure, so the horse over-reacts instead of responding calmly.

▷ You are applying too little pressure, so the aid isn't clear, and the horse can comfortably ignore it if he chooses.

▷ You are giving contradictory aids due to a lack of co-ordination on your part. For example, your hands are saying 'no' while your legs are saying 'go', creating confusion in the horse.

▷ You are continuing to apply pressure even when the horse has responded to the request, so he never finds himself in a comfort zone, making him sour. His way of saving himself from this frustration is often to become 'dead' to the aids. Everyone wants some sort of feedback when they've completed a task, for better or for worse.

▷ You are setting the horse inappropriate tasks for his ability or training. Imagine you're trying to teach a young child football. You start with the goalposts really wide and may even move them slightly to facilitate his success. If he constantly fails to score he will become disillusioned, if he constantly succeeds, however, he will become apathetic and it's time to narrow the posts to increase the difficulty.

▷ You are applying ineffective aids so that the horse switches off and becomes unresponsive. While you must always give the horse the chance to respond to a polite request first time round, you should reserve the right to ask less politely the second time if he ignores you, that means you should back up your aid in an appropriate way, say with a wip-wop or a firm voice command. **Note:** your aim in doing this is to explain more clearly what you want, and is very different to 'punishing' a horse. A jab in the mouth and a boot in the ribs is not a logical explanation to a horse that has run out at a fence, for example. A smack on the shoulder he is trying to run out through *at the time he is doing it* might be.

Remember, the rider can both prevent and correct mistakes in the horse. The horse only learns from the latter.

Advanced techniques

Once you've got a well-balanced and obedient horse, which not only responds immediately to pressure but even starts to anticipate it, you're really in a position to start having fun! Think of different ways to test the system and stimulate your horse's mind and body into greater subtlety of communication. For example, one of my horse Pelo's party tricks is to be ridden without a bridle. It's a great test of trust and communication for both of us. He understands the concept of pressure and release so well we can jump, hack, gallop, without a bridle – in fact, he almost goes better without one. Perhaps it's because I have to be more intuitive as a rider, and the subtle form of communication suits his intelligence and character.

Pelo came to me as a problem horse. He was very suspicious of everything that was asked of him; he couldn't stand a bit in his mouth and would rather throw himself on the floor than do as he was asked. Pelo's behaviour now is the result of three years' work: he has taught me more than any other horse, and it is my success with him that has given me faith in these methods. If it works on an animal as difficult and sceptical as he was, it'll work on most horses! It's also proof that you cannot solve a problem over night, but time and patience will win the day in most cases.

GIVE TO PRESSURE

A loop of rope around Pelo's nose has the same effect as a bit or bridle. He gives to the pressure and turns his head.

PREPARATION IS IMPORTANT

Here I am reminding Pelo of what pressure on the neck means in preparation for riding without a bridle, the ultimate test of his understanding and my training.

UNBRIDLED TRUTH

I discovered Pelo's ability without the bridle by chance. I was in the school one day, messing about, 'practising what I preach' you might say, and he was going beautifully. Into my head popped the saying, 'When you take away all the equipment you will be left with the truth', so I decided to take this to an extreme and really take away all the equipment, including the bridle. What I was left with was unbelievable. Pelo was responsive, engaged, balanced and forward. I even got the feeling that he preferred to go without a bit, and to this day, riding and jumping him without a bridle is a key part of many of my demonstrations.

MAKING THE LINK WITH RIDDEN WORK

As part of Pelo's preparation for riding without a bridle, I've got a halfway house – he's wearing a bridle but I'm really only using the strap and rein to neck rein him, not the bit.

PERFECT UNDERSTANDING LEADS TO HARMONY

If it has become second nature to the horse to give to pressure, he should do so regardless of where the pressure comes from. So let's remove all physical connection with the horse's head and see what happens. With just a piece of rope around the neck, I can apply as much pressure as I need to direct the horse, stop, start, turn and rein back. Note Pelo is technically 'on the bit' and completely balanced, controlled and engaged, but with no bit in sight! This really puts my previous training to the test. This is a horse in true self-carriage, which he has developed through several months of groundwork without a rider.

A JUMP AHEAD

My work with Pelo has led to us having a fantastic understanding. The fact that we are safely jumping without a bridle reveals the depth of his sensitivity to pressure, yet Pelo came to me as a real 'problem' horse who just had not responded to traditional training techniques.

Checklist for success

You will know when your training has been successful because your relationship with your horse and his attitude towards you will have changed out of all recognition from how it was when you began.

▷ Your horse has accepted responsibility for keeping rhythm, impulsion, alignment and carriage on a given pattern or line, through all paces and transitions.

▷ Your horse appears self-motivated and peaceful in his expression.

▷ You can travel passively on the movement because your horse understands delegation.

▷ You are able to use sophisticated aiding, implicit gestures rather than explicit actions.

▷ You can 'give' the rein to test self-carriage.

▷ Your horse stays light in the hand through turns and transitions.

▷ Your horse will willingly carry out the next instruction because he is physically able to do so.

▷ Your horse may think ahead of you. In other words, he'll have the kettle on before you've asked for that cup of tea!

Problems and problem horses

Can't or won't?

Problems in horses *never* come from nowhere, and eliminating them is often just a matter of patiently working back to the real root of the problem – not the symptom, which is usually difficult behaviour or under performance – but the cause. The more patient and generous the horse is, the longer it may take you to unravel the years of compensatory behaviour that hide the true cause.

All bad behaviour is the horse trying to escape pressure, whether it's physical, mental or emotional. What you need to determine is whether it's true evasion, or simply the horse trying to find a solution to the position he's in. There are the obvious cases of abuse and neglect that might cause bad behaviour. But life may also get pretty oppressive for those equine athletes that do the same job day in and day out because we demand it of them, or those that are subject to a management routine which suits our needs rather than theirs, as well as those that suffer from pain that they can't communicate to us.

As I've explained throughout this book, when training a horse, my preference, and hopefully that of most horse people, is to reward good behaviour. Rewards vary from the physical to the mental and emotional, too. A comfort zone for the horse isn't just a pat or a carrot, it's also the company of other horses, removal of the rider's weight, return to a physically less demanding exercise, the softening of a rein, even your attention in an unexpected form. Believe it or not, shouting or throwing a brush at the horse when

he kicks his stable door may be just what he wants.

HOW'S HE FEELING

There are signs that reveal how your horse is feeling, and a thinking rider should use them to find out whether his behaviour stems from disobedience or discomfort. His ears will tell you where his attention is, so you want at least one trained on you as you school. Look particularly for the flick of an ear when you apply an aid or issue a different instruction, and see how long it takes from flicker to response.

Look also for a loose floppy lip and chin, soft, round nostrils and a loose, relaxed tail. When there is tension in any of these areas, the associated flight hormones are also released and the horse is physiologically not in a position to work well for you.

To generalize broadly, if the horse shows every sign of being relaxed when he is misbehaving and makes several threats before he actually does something wrong, he is probably being disobedient. If the behaviour occurs suddenly and is accompanied by signs of tension such as tight nostrils, a clamped tail

WON'T!
Troy is an experienced competition horse who has got used to doing things his own way, here he's avoiding contact.

and tight chin, then he's more likely to be afraid or in pain. If you're concentrating on staying on board, you may not be in a position to observe these tell-tale signs, so ask a friend to observe or see if you can get the behaviour on video. Better still, work the horse from the ground and see if it occurs then.

Once you've observed the signs, you need to get to the root of your horse's discomfort – physical, mental or emotional – and solve that.

PHYSICAL PRESSURE

Your horse lives under conditions quite different from those found in the wild. His diet and the demands made on his body are largely unnatural. Radio-tracking studies of mustangs show that they travel an average of 30–40 miles a day throughout the year as a natural consequence of their search for food and water. The impact of confinement on domestic horses has been well documented. For example, they may be more stressed, their legs, feet and respiration may suffer, and they will have a higher parasite load. The domestic lifestyle can result in a lack of physical well-being that results in bad behaviour, simply because the horse is trying to tell you something.

Where there is no obvious bleeding, swelling, cut, heat or

> The vast majority of horses I see (even the well-behaved ones) have a degree of physical discomfort that is stopping them performing to their full potential.

lameness, it can be hard to convince owners that their horse is actually in pain. However, the vast majority of horses I see (even the well-behaved ones) have a degree of physical discomfort that is stopping them performing to their full potential. The kindest and most generous horses are usually the worst off, as they try to please in spite of it, and put up with whatever is asked of them. Those who end up in my yard as unrideable are generally the more sensitive ones who simply refuse to go along with it any more.

Blatant signs of physical discomfort are bucking, rearing, bolting, stopping at fences and other behaviours commonly misread as

PASSIVE STRETCHING

You can help your horse stay physically well with correct riding and school-ing, along with passive stretches, which you can do yourself. Passive stretching is an important part of keeping your horse supple and alerting you to any early warning signs of discomfort or restriction in movement.

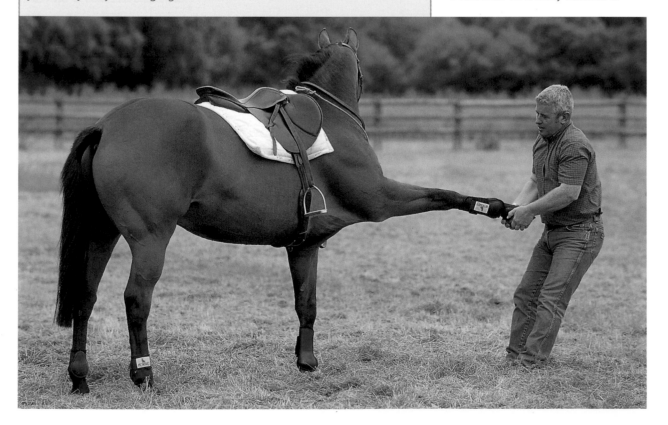

Tips for Problem Solving

▷ Try to see the situation from your horse's point of view. Think about what you are doing and what your horse is trying to tell you.

▷ Try again, take a different approach, do anything except lose your temper. Some horses take weeks or even months to respond to positive reinforcement, and the amount required varies, too. Increase the pressure until you get a response, but beware of going past the point where horse is willing to respond. If you escalate pressure unfairly, your horse may escalate the undesired behaviour.

▷ Become aware of very small changes in behaviour. Be ready to support and guide the horse at that very early stage. In this way the problem won't be able to escalate.

▷ Be logical. For horses to feel comfortable and respond the way you want them to, everything you do needs to be in black and white, with no grey areas. If you build up logically from small beginnings, you will always have a solid area to step back to if you get into trouble. However, you also need to respect the horse's intelligence and make sure that you are giving him enough to think about.

▷ Look at yourself. Generally, horses don't disobey; they obey what we've unknowingly taught them. If you're not getting the results you want, check that you are being logical, precise and consistent, and that you follow every response to pressure with the reward – immediate release.

▷ Don't 'show him who's boss'. You need to be assertive, but being aggressive can give out the wrong signals. In the horse world, true leaders aren't bullies (see p.27). Lead by example, not force.

▷ Be as consistent as possible from one day to the next. This means that if somebody else is working with your horse and doing something he isn't comfortable or familiar with, stop them. Stand up for your horse!

---

schooling problems. More subtle signs might be trickier to recognize: a reluctance to load due to finding difficulty with a steep ramp or balance within the vehicle, for example, or misbehaving with the farrier as he attempts to manipulate and stretch the limbs.

Some of the more common things that are overlooked are: areas of the neck, back or tail being sore to even just fingertip pressure; flinching, impatience or restlessness when being rugged or saddled; increased nervousness on one side compared to the other; reduced range of motion in a limb; decreased flexion in a joint; head tossing or stumbling when ridden; refusal to go forward or being too speedy.

The more tense the horse is, the more he feels pain. The more

frightened he is, the more likely he is to perceive that he is feeling pain, even though what we are doing wouldn't affect another horse in the same physical condition. Conversely, adrenalin can also make the horse less sensitive to pain – as in the horse that resents schooling but is fine at shows or on hacks. People often deduce that if the horse behaves well in one situation then he must 'having you on' when he's difficult in another, but this isn't necessarily the case.

Only an expert can solve real physical problems: as well as having a good vet, every horse owner needs to work alongside a competent farrier, saddler, equine dentist (see also pp.122–124) and equine physiotherapist/chiropractor to keep their horse mentally and physically comfortable and content.

ELIMINATE PAIN

When I am sent problem horses, I first eliminate any pain by using the relevant expert, then I start to re-train from the ground. I do this for two main reasons:

1 Horses don't understand that once the cause of the pain is removed it won't hurt: you have to *show them* that it no longer hurts.

2 By long lining you can get the horse to work forward and correctly, so re-building under-developed muscles without the added weight of the rider.

Once any physical problems have been addressed you will be faced with the problem of repairing the psychological damage – convincing the horse that it's OK to relax as the source of his discomfort has now gone, perhaps after many years: this is where groundwork and distance training become invaluable, as well as a great deal of patience. I find it takes about 3–4 weeks of long lining work to see a big difference (see 'Eliminate pain', p.119) and then, when the horse is going forward in a confident manner and he looks stronger, I introduce the rider again.

MENTAL AND EMOTIONAL PRESSURE

Do we get over sentimental about our horses? And can it affect the way we train them? Most of us believe we observe all sorts of emotion in our horses: fear, anxiety, loneliness, happiness. Is there any scientific basis for this or are we just imagining it? Whatever the answer, given that horses do not 'fake' being sick or sorry, we are right to note any apparent emotions because if a horse seems 'depressed' or unhappy there is likely to be a physical reason for it (see above and pp.122–125).

The emotional life of animals has been a controversial subject for centuries and continues to be so. One of the reasons behavioural scientists find it difficult to study emotion and consciousness in animals is that it's hard to describe subjective mental experiences with enough precision to allow objective testing. However, when humans and other animals were examined using brain scans, they showed similar activity in parts of the brain believed to be involved in emotion. The limbic system, which is

WATCH AND LEARN

Looking at Pelo, it is clear that he is having a great time. Take the trouble to watch your horse – at work and play – and learn what he really enjoys. It will give you ideas on how to reward him when he does well.

thought to control emotion, is one of the oldest parts of the brain in evolutionary development. This means that it is found in a variety of species. Also shared are certain substances such as oxytocin, seretonin and testosterone, which are believed to affect the feelings and actions of humans. Given this physical congruence, it seems unlikely that we are the only species with the capacity to feel emotion.

What is certain is that horses have the naturally nervous disposition appropriate to a flight animal, and, as such, are poorly designed to cope with stress. Left to themselves, they would graze all day surrounded by the comfort and security of their friends, and go out of their way to avoid any pressures. There's little doubt among behaviourists that domestic living can place all kinds of stresses on a horse's health, leading to

abnormal behaviour. In stabled horses this may result in what is called a stereotypy or 'vice'. I have found that a lot of horses seem to develop vices to deal with a certain situation and then trying to stop the vice can cause them more stress. For example, my old head groom, Lucy Emerick, had a fantastic event horse, but he cribbed like mad, so we put a collar on him; within two days he had serious colic. A few days after he came home, we put the collar back on, and again he went down with colic. We realized that by stopping the vice we were causing him more stress. I appreciate that something must have triggered the vice to start with, but that's

beside the point, he had the vice and we just had to learn to live with it.

If your horse is not coping, mentally or emotionally, with what you are asking usually, he will show his insecurity by taking every opportunity to be back in the safety of 'the herd' such as spinning round, napping, rearing, jogging home, refusing to load, bad behaviour at shows. You name it, he'll try it. He's not necessarily being 'naughty' although this is often how it comes across. As far as he is concerned, it's a matter of life and death because he doesn't trust you as herd leader and feels the need to take decisions into his own hands (see p.27). The most

important thing you can do for your horse is to make sure that he feels safe – physically and emotionally – in your company. This trust will only come if you are the respected herd leader and he knows you will act in his best interests.

Every horse needs a varied exercise routine that is within his physical capabilities, including fun activities that he enjoys, even if they're not usually part of your agenda, such as a good gallop or a hack in company. If you have used groundwork to build his trust and simplify his training into a logical and progressive system, then there is no reason why he shouldn't be mentally and emotionally settled. Some horses, like some humans, are simply more highly strung and emotional than others. You need to tap into your horse's personality and be quick to decide what his type is so you can react appropriately to cajole, reassure or scold as necessary.

Equine dental health
by GREG WOOD

Your horse is having problems eating, maybe you have problems putting in the bit, perhaps you've noticed his teeth are a bit on the sharp side – time to call out your equine dentist. Well yes, these are the obvious reasons why people think their horse may have discomfort in his mouth. But there are many other problems that develop as a result of poor dental health, and they get overlooked every time.

We are a nation of animal lovers and our horses must come out at the top, or very close to the top, of the list of pampered pets. And yet, we still constantly overlook a fundamental aspect of their health, which will have a direct effect on their behaviour and performance – their teeth. We are not an ignorant people, but it is vital that we get more education in this area if we are to get the optimum out of our, let's face it, very expensive hobby.

CHOOSING A DENTIST

Unfortunately, there are lots of people who claim to be dentists but the quality of their work is low. Beware. The dentist should treat the horse with a combination of discipline and kindness, have a clean and cared for set of instruments and equipment, should explain his procedures to you and allow you to feel the horse's teeth before and after treatment. He or she should always use a full mouth speculum or gag to allow safe access to the horse's entire mouth, which extends quite some way back in the jaw. This is not a device to pry or force open the mouth but simply holds it comfortably after the horse willingly opens it. Equine dentists may work alone or in conjunction with a vet. It is highly recommended that you get a qualified specialist.

WHAT TO EXPECT

Charges are based on the type of work performed. You can expect to pay a vet's call-out fee, a fee for treatment, and cost of drugs administered if any. Here are some possible services:

▷ Examination, evaluation and consultation
▷ Educational demonstrations
▷ Removal of wolf teeth

BASIC ANATOMY OF THE HORSE'S HEAD

To understand how important teeth are, we need to look at the basic anatomy of the horse's head and the biomechanics of the horse (how it functions) in relation to teeth.

Temporomandibular joint (TMJ)

molars

premolars

wolf tooth

tushes or canines

incisors

lower mandible

HAS MY HORSE GOT A PROBLEM WITH ITS TEETH?

WHEN RIDDEN
▷ Head throwing problems
▷ Head tilting
▷ Change in ridden performance
▷ Poor performance
▷ Hard to bit
▷ Rearing
▷ Hanging tongue out of mouth or putting tongue over the bit

WHEN EATING
▷ Head tilting
▷ Bolting food
▷ Quidding (dribbling feed)
▷ Eating hay before hard food
▷ Change in drinking habits
▷ Choking

GENERAL APPEARANCE
▷ Discharge from the eye or nose
▷ Teeth sensitive to the touch when palpating from the outer cheek area
▷ Excessive salivation or drooling
▷ Irregular movement of mandible
▷ Troubled expression
▷ Bad general attitude

▷ Inability to shift lower jaw from side to side
▷ Bad smell from mouth or nostrils
▷ Sores on the lips, gums, palate
▷ Bleeding from the mouth
▷ Bumps or enlargements on the jaw or face
▷ Fistulous discharge on jaw or face

▷ Large hooks on upper front molars
▷ Longer than normal particles in the faeces
▷ Weight loss
▷ Lack of condition, when all other good maintenance programmes are in place

▷ Pulling of caps (expired baby teeth)
▷ Floating (grinding off sharp points)
▷ Cutting and smoothing canines
▷ Removal of plaque build up from canines
▷ Performance floating, such as a bit seat
▷ Incisor adjustment (shortening long incisors or reshaping incisors which have worn more on one side than the other, thus unbalancing the mouth)
▷ Cut hooks from fore and aft ends of cheek batteries
▷ Occlusal table adjustment (grinding off uneven edges and re-shaping grinding surfaces of cheek teeth)

TEETHING

The foal is born with 12 premolars: six upper and six lower. His incisors will start to emerge at intervals, the first erupting at 6–8 days, more following at 6–8 weeks, and finally corner incisors appearing at 6–8 months.

The premolars and the incisors are deciduous teeth, referred to as 'caps'. They are eventually replaced by permanent teeth. Problems can occur when caps are retained, and may become noticeable when youngsters are started, such as during bitting. Regular dental checks (every 5–6 months) should be made to ensure that the permanent teeth are erupting correctly. The discomfort of a retained cap can have a marked effect on a horse's behaviour and performance.

Next to erupt are the wolf teeth, usually when the horse is between 6 and 18 months old. Wolf teeth are regularly confused with tushes or canines; there have been occasions when I have been told that the wolf teeth have already been removed, only to open the horse's mouth and find that his tushes are gone and his wolf teeth are in plain view. Ideally, wolf teeth should be removed before the horse starts his education as they can cause a lot of discomfort during bitting and later can cause head-shaking and rearing, among other problem behaviour.

Wolf teeth should only be taken out by a vet or a qualified equine dental technician, and with the horse sedated. This is the only humane way of doing it. The job must be done by a professional to avoid potentially fatal damage to the palatine artery in the roof of the mouth. In addition, it is easy to break wolf teeth and leave fragments in the jaw, which can be worse for the horse than the wolf tooth itself.

Molars start erupting at 12 months and tushes will normally appear at around 4½ years old.

THE TMJ

Biomechanics is an incredibly complex subject, too much to go into here, so I will only cover how the mandible and the temporomandibular joint (TMJ) works in order to explain why it affects performance. From a dental point of view, the TMJ is as important as the teeth.

When you watch a horse eat, the majority of the movement seems to be lateral (side-to-side), but the mandible also has some anterior and posterior (forward and backward) movement. The horse needs these various movements to function correctly, and they can be limited or restricted by problems with the teeth.

If you look at a horse's incisors, most will have a slight overbite (the upper incisors protrude slightly over the lower incisors), normally about 2–4mm. This is quite natural and should not be confused with a parrot mouth. The horse should spend most of his day with his head down, grazing: a wild horse will spend 16–18 hours a day like this. As his head goes down to graze, his mandible will come forward by 2–4mm, lining up the incisors so that the teeth can be used for nipping the grass. This also aligns the molars so that each tooth has one opposing it to grind the food. The grazing horse uses the full range of movement through the mandible.

Now consider the stabled horse; we often put its head in unnatural eating positions by using haynets, hay racks, raised mangers, and so on. Why do we do this? Is it for the horse or for our own convenience? By making them feed in this way we are completely changing the wear pattern of their teeth, creating various imbalances in the mouth, such as hooks and ramps (see below). These imbalances can have a detrimental effect on the TMJ, causing what is called TMJ pressure. Other dental abnormalities that can cause

TMJ pressure include wave mouth, shear mouth, overlong incisors and protruberant teeth.

A large percentage of horses with performance problems suffer from some degree of TMJ pressure. To understand what this is, grit your teeth together and hold for a while; the tightness you experience down the side of your face is a form of TMJ pressure.

DIAGNOSIS AND TREATMENT OF TMJ PAIN

TMJ pain is very common in the horse. A huge number of the horses I examine demonstrate some discomfort when this area is palpated. If you've ever tried to handle a horse that is unwilling to have his head touched, or shakes or jerks it, or is reluctant to do what he is asked, or is of a bad disposition, he probably has pain in the TMJ area. Treatment should be aimed at correcting dental abnormalities and so allowing painless movement of the TMJ.

The way I check for TMJ health is thus: the mandible must have anterior and posterior movement (this is tested with the mouth closed). Also, I look for good lateral movement, which allows the horse to eat correctly. A horse should not object to moderate pressure to the TMJ area, so one with a painful TMJ will respond by pulling its head away or throwing its head up. Many horses that are sore in the TMJ are also sore around the poll and atlas area.

In most cases, horses with a sore TMJ will change their gait and the way they carry themselves, to accommodate the problem. This misuse of the muscle groups can result in further problems through the neck, shoulders, back and hindquarters.

THE FUTURE

Horses have varying degrees of tolerance to pain: some can be suffering a great deal of discomfort in the TMJ but showing only slight symptoms, while others can be aggressive when handled, or rear, nap, buck, and so on when ridden.

I come across these cases regularly, but particularly when I work with Richard on horses that have established behavioural problems. I also receive calls to work on horses that have been through long expensive treatments from chiropractors and physiotherapists; the teeth are generally the last things to be checked. Unfortunately, any benefit to the horse through manipulating the mandible will be undone in a matter of hours if the teeth are not

---

HOOKS AND RAMPS

Among of the most common dental problems encountered are hooks and ramps. The hook is generally found on the first upper premolar and the ramp is located on the very back lower molar. Hooks and ramps can be caused by unnatural use of the mandible, as described above. The size of the hook or ramp will determine the amount of TMJ pressure experienced. However, the horse's overall demeanour and its tolerance to pain will also dictate the resulting effect on performance.

balanced beforehand. Therefore, it is encouraging to see professionals such as Richard ensure the teeth of all the horses that he works with are checked and balanced before he embarks on any other treatments.

Although it can cause so many problems, the TMJ is not usually addressed in examination for soundness. Advances in equine dentistry have increased our ability to recognize and treat these problems. Hopefully, this situation will continue improving with better diagnosis, prevention and treatment.

A DENTAL TIMETABLE

> CHECK AND FLOAT ALL HORSE'S TEETH AT LEAST TWICE A YEAR

EARLY YEARLINGS	EARLY 2-YEAR-OLD	LATE 2-YEAR-OLD (2½ YEARS)	EARLY 3-YEAR-OLD
▷ Float premolars	▷ Float premolars	▷ Float premolars	▷ Float premolars
	▷ Float permanent molars in occlusion	▷ Float permanent molars in occlusion	▷ Float permanent molars in occlusion
LATE YEARLINGS ▷ Float premolars	▷ Check eruption of first permanent molars	▷ Remove retained first premolar caps	▷ Remove retained second premolar caps
▷ Extract wolf teeth		▷ Check eruption of permanent molars	▷ Check eruption of second permanent molars
		▷ Check eruption of incisors	▷ Check eruption of incisors

LATE 3-YEAR-OLD (3½ YEARS)	EARLY 4-YEAR-OLD	LATE 4-YEAR-OLD (4½ YEARS)	5 YEARS AND ON
▷ Float premolars	▷ Float all molars	▷ Float all molars	▷ Routine floating and check ups at least twice a year
▷ Float permanent molars in occlusion	▷ Remove any retained molar caps	▷ Remove any retained molar caps	
▷ Remove retained second premolar caps	▷ Check eruption of third permanent molars	▷ Check eruption of third permanent molars	
▷ Check eruption of permanent molars	▷ Watch for retained cap slivers or splinters	▷ Check eruption of canines in male horses	
▷ Check eruption of incisors	▷ Watch for deciduous incisor root fragments	▷ Watch for blind canines in male horses	
▷ Remove retained second incisor caps		▷ Remove any retained third incisor caps	

Troubleshooting

First, some general advice related to the underlying factor in many problems, both ridden and from the ground: part of respecting a horse's instincts is understanding how they like to live. This also plays a big part in keeping them content and, therefore, co-operative, and preventing abnormal or difficult behaviour occurring. I've already discussed how stressed horses do not, and often cannot, perform well. Hence the cases of horses doing well at home but becoming upset at shows. But how are some horses able to rise above these problems? How can you build calm confidence in an animal whose evolution dictates he needs to be a highly excitable character to survive? Horses that have become socially dysfunctional though unnatural management are particularly unlikely to acquit themselves well. Those that live a psychologically 'healthy' lifestyle at home cope far better. Being allowed plenty of time to live in a comparatively natural state at grass and in the company of other horses is highly beneficial for a horse's mental and physical well-being, and the impact this can have on their behaviour should not be underestimated.

If it's not nipped in the bud, something that starts as high jinks can become an annoying habit.

Ridden problems and solutions

My horse ... is dead to the leg

A horse's responses become dull either because he hasn't had the pressure-release theory explained to him properly in the first place, or because his desire to fulfil his part of the bargain has been lost. This usually happens when a horse isn't rewarded with immediate release when he responds to pressure and does as he was asked – in other words, the rider or handler keeps 'nagging', so the horse starts to wonder, what's in it for me? And under those circumstances, of course, the answer is 'nothing'. Many horses that are apparently 'dead to the leg' have become so because they are highly sensitive and, as a form of self-defence from its constant nagging, they have blocked it out.

This is a very common problem and creates a vicious circle. The rider has to use more and more leg and hand to elicit an ever-diminishing response. From there, many see the only possible step forward to be whips and spurs. Although I am not anti whips and spurs – they have their place – if that's the only way you can get your horse to listen to you then his respect is for the whips and spurs and not you as a rider.

SOLUTION You need to find a different stimulus – not the same stimulus, repeated more forcefully – and change the usual format of your schooling to reawaken the horse's interest. You need to be absolutely certain that he is rewarded for positive behaviour. Check out the section on developing subtlety (pp.94–95).

The focus is on getting him to go forward – never mind the rein contact! This is why I dislike the phrase 'on the bit' as it puts the rider's attention on the horse's forehand and implies that the solution to the perfect outline lies in the connection with their hands and the horse's mouth. In fact, their attention should be on the 'engine' behind them, and the connection between their legs and the horse's back and hindquarters.

My horse ... is very spooky

SOLUTION Apart from the obvious method of allowing the horse to get used to scary objects and build his confidence from day one, the answer to this is much the same as above. It's very common for a horse that is dead to the leg to be very spooky, too, which can surprise people but in fact makes perfect sense in horse terms. It's partly because he does not trust his rider enough to be confident and assured, partly because he is not enjoying his work and

is looking for excuses, and partly because he really is in his own world most if the time and gets taken by surprise!

You want your horse's mental attention and focus, so that he is working with you and listening, rather than being 'away with the fairies' and doing his own thing. Draw his attention away from the scary object by working with the wip-wop (p.95). Just something to bear in mind, if a horse has a trapped nerve or is in physical pain, it can make him hyper-sensitive to things that wouldn't normally bother him.

My horse ... is heavy in the hand

When you are riding and you feel that dull ache between your shoulder blades, your horse is using you as a fifth leg! This is a classic problem with a horse that is not in self-carriage. He is relying on you to carry him, so don't let him. He must stop looking for rein support, and learn to stretch forward and down, in all paces. Make sure he's being given freedom to do this; it may take him a while to take it, but at least the offer is there. Yes, he may be dying for something to lean on, but he will never carry himself if you constantly support him. (Read about my work with Pelo, pp.108–113, to understand that a horse doesn't need any bit at all to hold himself correctly.)

SOLUTION Go back to your groundwork and use rope circling and long lines until your horse learns to carry himself without a rider, then build up his strength and good habits under saddle by getting 'forward' before all else. The forehand will lighten in front as the back-end engages, and only in that order.

Ask your horse to go forward into trot in a safe environment. When he gets heavy in the hand, drop the contact. He will probably wobble all over the place, because he isn't balanced. The other thing he will do is trip frequently, again this is because he isn't balanced and is used to you propping him up. When you feel the time is right and he's working more by himself, pick up the contact; as soon as you feel him leaning again, drop the contact. Gradually the tripping will become less and the time between the corrections will get longer.

My horse ... tanks off

SOLUTION Look at the exercise where you bring the horse's head round to your knee (p.99). This comes in really handy if you have a horse that tanks off or bolts. Think of your horse's head and neck as an arrow: when it is straight it can go a long way and quickly, but if you were to bend the arrow it wouldn't be able to go anywhere. Bending your horse's neck in this way 'disengages' him so he can't tank off.

In a safe environment, preferably fenced, see whether your horse can do the exercise of bending his neck around to your knee at halt. (If he can't, don't put him in a situation where he might tank off. It's like taking your car to the shops even though you know your brakes are dodgy!) Once you have your horse flexible and doing what you ask in halt, ask him to go forward, first in walk. Take him across the diagonal and let one rein go, then pick up the other rein and think about drawing your hand to the middle of your chest, remembering – upward pressure not backward pressure. As soon as he bends his neck to your knee, he will stop going forward. When he stands, rub his face and tell him he is a good boy. Ask him to go forward again. Repeat this exercise every now and again in your schooling session. When he is responding well in walk, ask for it in trot and so on.

If you have a horse that tanks off have him carefully checked to eliminate any physical reasons for the behaviour, such as teeth, back and tack. If there was a physical problem, once it is removed you should find that with ground training, you see a huge drop in this type of behaviour and the bending exercise will help you to have more control over it.

My horse ... is one-sided

The vast majority of horses are one-sided, so the rider needs to bear this in mind and be sympathetic while the horse develops equal strength and dexterity. Continually working more on the weak side is not the answer; it just creates soreness and resentment and thus confirms in the horse's mind that it is uncomfortable and will make him want to do it even less.

SOLUTION Make it as easy as possible for the horse to grasp a different concept by starting new lessons on the good side for say, 80 per cent of the time, then work the weaker side for the other 20 per cent and build up until you reach an equal 50 per cent of time spent on each side. This work is best done on long lines. Trot him on his good side for about 2–3 minutes then turn him onto his stiff side. You will find he doesn't want to turn but be quiet and persistent with your outside line and once he has turned, walk him for 30 seconds, turn him back onto his good side and trot for 2–3 minutes again. Keep repeating this until he offers to turn onto his stiff side. You can then start to ask a little bit more until you are getting equal work on both reins. Remember it won't happen overnight, and don't long line for more than 20 minutes at a time (see p.73).

My horse ... behaves badly at shows

A very common problem and really demoralizing for the owner is the horse that is generally fine at home but lets itself down at shows or public outings. If anything, the harder you try, the worse it gets. Often the behaviour is due to chronic attention seeking or insecurity. Using bad behaviour to attract attention is an old trick in the equine book. No amount of calming supplements, different feeds, alternative therapies or particular ways of preparing and working in at shows will make a real difference until you tackle this. Remember that apparently confident and bolshy behaviour is often just the horse being defensive and looking for someone to take control. Showing him 'who's boss' will also make things worse.

SOLUTION First, look for the obvious – do you use different tack or special equipment at shows, or feed your horse something different beforehand for whatever reason? Eliminate these possible causes first. Then address the insecurity issue by giving the horse a cast-iron work routine, which you can use to settle him at the showground. What you need is a tool you can take anywhere and use to diffuse the situation without putting yourself or anyone else in danger. I prefer long lining to lungeing for this because it's more interactive and the two lines of communication direct to the bit give a better representation of what happens when you ride, so the horse can translate what he learns more easily to ridden work.

Use the long lining before mounting, every time you ride. This will give you a barometer of his mood. If he's bolshy keep doing it until he calms down. It might take 5 minutes or 20; you may even decide you're not going to ride if he's being really difficult. Let him know that you're just not going to participate when he's in that sort of mood. This is especially important if in the past you've taken him on and he's won the battle. He can take it out on the long reins instead of you, then he is effectively fighting himself.

Do long lining exercises every day during the build up to a show, then for as long as it takes to get him relaxed and attentive before you mount prior to the class. Keep to a rock solid routine when you arrive at a showground so he knows exactly what to expect, and what is expected of him, every time.

When the improvement becomes obvious to you, take the opportunity to change your behaviour and regain the upper hand. Think of changing your riding dialogue from 'No, don't do that' to the more positive 'I'd like this now' or 'Could you try that?' so he stays interested and doesn't feel it's up to him to take the decisions. Of course, you can't let a horse do his own thing all the time, but it's demoralizing for him to be always told, 'No, stop that'. Being responsible for his actions is not the same as being allowed to take over.

My horse ... gets excited when jumping

Excited through pleasure, or stressed through pain, misunderstanding or lack of confidence? The signs can be very similar and people often get these confused. How you deal with it depends on the cause.

SOLUTION Assuming it's not a pain issue, the first step is for your horse to develop a more comfortable and correct way of going. When this happens his shoulders will be freer and he find jumping easier, setting up a 'virtuous circle'.

Many horses that find jumping stressful or exciting, hollow their back and throw their head up and the rider needs to overcome his or her natural reaction to try pinning it down with a strong, low hand, and do just the opposite. Play the horse at his own game and lift your hand to match the horse's head carriage in motion (see p.98). Remember, you are simply trying to make the right thing comfortable and the wrong thing uncomfortable. A still, soft contact is your horse's reward. Horses that are not carrying themselves forward in a balanced way almost encourage you to shorten the rein and fiddle because they want you to help them! Yes, you are the decision maker, but it's the horse that must have the confidence and willingness to assess the fence and get you both over it.

If you find your horse is unbalanced, go back to working on long lines to help to lengthen the distance between his chin and chest; his jumping will be helped by the additional movement through his neck and back muscles as he relaxes into a longer outline, propels himself forward from the hindquarters and lengthens his stride.

If you just can't stop yourself fiddling or suspect an uneven contact is making matters worse, ride with the reins in one hand to make it impossible.

If your horse frequently knocks fences, jumping ability is rarely the problem unless you're competing at a high level. It's more usually the horse's inability to maintain a slow rhythm and use himself properly on the approach, and these classic signs of an unbalanced horse will also be reflected in your flat work. You know the answer – develop self-carriage with rope circling and long lining!

Check out your own riding: many people make the mistake of riding differently because they're jumping. Doing nothing can be very difficult! Keep the energy contained and think: canter, carriage, containment.

Personally, I'm not a fan of the placing poles and similar tricks. They're fine for teaching youngsters, but in this sort of case they are a trick to help you get over the fence and you won't have that help at an event. Put the time and effort into developing a horse that is mentally and physically agile, and you'll probably find many of your problems disappear.

Make sure you do your work at home – you don't want to be going to an event hoping all will be well. If the problem is very bad it might be money well spent to enlist the help of a professional.

My horse ... is nappy

If your horse is unhappy to go it alone for any reason, as ever begin by assessing whether there is any physical reason why he should misbehave. Nappiness not related to pain and associated with riding often develops through a need to dominate. It makes perfect sense even if the horse is easy in every other respect, such as when you are tacking up. There's no reason for him not to be amenable at this stage, because he knows that he is in charge and that when it comes to it, he'll only do as much or as little as he wants to anyway. As you start to regain control in your ridden work, you might find he becomes less co-operative about being caught as he starts to realize that he is not in charge any more. The ridden problem is an effect of the dominance, not a cause, and it will improve as the horse becomes generally more submissive.

SOLUTION The first step in regaining attention and respect is, of course, to use the training halter as described in part one (pp.46–51), then increasing the distance with rope circling (pp.64–69). Subsequently, long reining work (pp.74–79) will allow you to deal with evasions safely, as you have control of the horse's quarters. This will also have a huge psychological effect as you can make him do as he's told without any danger to yourself. During this work, expect the horse to try every evasion in the book as he realizes that he is no longer in control. The evasions will probably reflect exactly what he does under saddle: throwing his head about, backing up, charging round, bucking, rearing. Don't prevent or punish any of this, but don't allow him to stop working either. All this is habitual behaviour, and he'll soon realize he's putting far more effort into it than he needs to.

Spend as much time as it takes on the groundwork until you are totally confident about your ability to control movement and direction again. The first ridden work should follow a successful ground session and be short and sweet – ask for the same submissive actions as you have done on the ground, such as rein back, stepping the quarters away, moving the shoulders, then stop for the day.

It's common sense to repeat the elements that worked on the ground until they work on top too, and remember that when a horse is mentally stimulated, he usually forgets to be naughty. By using the same tactics of getting the horse to move away from pressure, stepping sideways, backwards and forwards, you'll find you are back on the ladder of co-operation. If you encounter problems at any stage, be quick to take a step back to the groundwork until you are back on a firm footing again, from which to try a little more each day.

Dominant horses can be very difficult and sometimes even dangerous, so don't think you'll only solve the problem by taking a risk and riding. Make sure you are always the one who makes the decision to stop working, and take that decision wisely, sooner rather than later – don't push the horse to a point where he is misbehaving again and you're forced to give up or start again. The wip-wop (p.95) can also be an invaluable tool in getting the nappy horse to think forwards, as it doesn't seem to create the same resentment as using a whip.

Pay attention to every detail, such as stopping with the horse facing away from direction he wants to go. Dominant horses are looking to take a mile for every inch you give, so make sure you don't give them a single one. It's also essential to take your discipline back to the stable with you. Making the horse step over and back up out of your space in every aspect of his life really will make a difference in the long term. However, avoid 'instructing' the horse all the time. This creates a situation where you're always reacting to him and thus he is still controlling you, rather than you making it clear you expect him to get on with things by himself until you say otherwise.

CASE HISTORY... My horse backs off the hand

Troy is now a teenager and has been a successful competition horse. He presents a pretty enough picture as long as you don't push him out of his accustomed way of doing things!

1 He holds himself in a rigid outline tucking his nose to his chest. The cramping of his neck muscles is clearly visible (right) despite very little contact from the rider.

2 If she pushes the rein forwards (left), he won't take it, and pokes his nose instead.

3 Any attempt to 'place' him in an outline results in the temper tantrums you can see (right) .

4 Troy is very unwilling to stretch forward and down. This is usually a defensive posture in a horse. He'll hold himself stiff and high to protect himself for a number of reasons, which may include an unsympathetic rein contact, incorrect bitting, physiological soreness or sharp teeth.

...steps to improvement

Start at the beginning, even with a horse as experienced as this. Troy's rider has to learn to refuse his invitation to take up the contact and keep asking for forward activity until he relaxes. In such a situation you must avoid double negatives at all costs: in this case, if you put your leg on, you want the horse to go forward, so don't take up a strong contact and discourage him from doing so. Rein contact is a refinement that comes later, but at this stage, the horse isn't ready for it. Keep it simple.

1 Troy begins rope circling after his initial introduction to the pressure halter (see pp.46–50). His habitual posture is clear to see when he starts off.

2 Given the freedom to experiment, he eventually tentatively tries dropping his nose and stretching his back. Hopefully, he'll quickly realize how good this feels compared to what he's been doing before.

CASE HISTORY... My horse backs off the hand (continued)

3 Next we progress to long lines. History repeats itself! On the long lines, Troy initially goes back to his defensive posture. Don't be disheartened if you feel every time you take a step forward, there's another one back. It's quite a normal pattern and doesn't mean the horse isn't learning. If you are patient and have firmly established the previous lessons, you'll see the evidence coming through as happens here.

4 There's no real surprises in his first outline – he's very reluctant to take the rein forward and down initially, which is an exact reflection of what he does under saddle. Left to work it out and with no rider to do it for him or fight against, plus the new stimulus of the long lines positioned in such a way as to guide him to a 'better place', he soon finds a posture that he should find comfortable enough to want to maintain for longer periods.

Hands up. The 'hands up' exercise (see p.98) is invaluable for Troy. Every time he throws his head up, the hands come with him.

5 Although this is not a 'good' outline in so far as it is flat and disengaged, it is at least relaxed and shows that Troy has changed his attitude to life in the last 20 minutes. It's a starting point on which we can improve; compare it with the first pictures of him where he is so tense and hyper, there was nothing to work with. Compare the shape and 'geography' of his neck muscles, too.

...steps to relaxation

6 Five minutes later and Troy has improved yet more. This time it's me on board and I've changed the bit to my preferred one – the Myler combination (inset). I find it works well on horses that are fussy about the bit pressure and schooled to pressure and release, as the noseband comes into action before the bit.

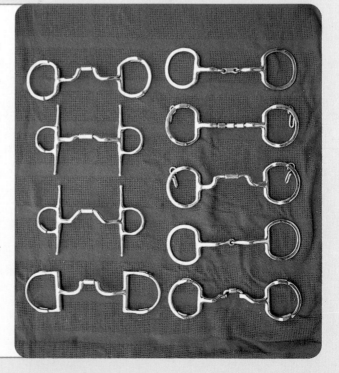

7 This is a revelation to Troy – he really can get his nose right down there! The expression on his face shows that he has found the session mentally tiring even though he is quite fit. It's not about working harder so much as working differently and more effectively.

MYLER BITS

The wide range of Myler bits means that you can choose one which reflects your ability and your horse's level of training and then progress to more advanced designs. Although you can stick with a Myler bit for schooling and hacking, you can't use them in some competitions such as dressage, but it is simple to make the transition to a conventional bit if necessary: horses find it much easier to swap from a Myler to a snaffle than from a pelham to a snaffle, for example.

CASE HISTORY... My horse is on the forehand

These pictures show Joe as relaxed but flat on the forehand. How can we change this way of going without 40 minutes of 'schooling' and lots of 'bump and grind' from the rider?

1&2 Although he is working in a long and low outline, at trot and canter Joe looks too much like he's going downhill, he's so much on the forehand. He needs to be persuaded to use his 'engine' by bringing his hind legs under his body.

3 It is easy to see how long lining work has encouraged Joe to engage his hind legs. This is the route to self-carriage and greater collection under saddle, but he has to learn to do it without the rider first.

...steps to engagement

4 Next make the connection to ridden work. After just 10 minutes of long lining the pair present a much better picture. Horse and rider are in a 'virtuous circle' where the rider can be quiet and subtle because the horse is being light, balanced and co-operative.

CASE HISTORY... My horse is crooked

Here's Troy again. Although his ridden work has improved (see pp.134–137), there is still some fine-tuning to be done.

1 From this picture, you can see that even when I'm showing him an open rein to the right, he is still tilting his nose to the left. This gives me good reason to suspect he will be crooked in motion, too.

2 I'm proved right when I take off all aids and sit still, just to see what will happen when Troy is allowed to canter a 'straight' line without any interference – he is far from straight.

3 Troy has trained his rider. She is working hard to keep him straight and prevent his quarters doing what she knows they habitually do, which is to swing left. In doing so she has collapsed to the left herself. I have asked her not to correct the quarters and she believes that she is not using her left leg at this point. This is a great example of how horses 'train' us into riding them exactly as they want to be ridden.

4 As with any problem, we start with groundwork. In this case, it will mobilize Troy's shoulders and engage his hind legs equally, which will help to develop the foundation of physical co-ordination and equality needed to correct his ridden work.

...steps to going straighter

5 When we make the connection to ridden work, it is clear that the groundwork has begun to pay off and we have a much straighter horse. To straighten a horse, don't correct the swing of the quarters with the leg, put the shoulders in front of the quarters with the rein, even if it means you drift away from the boards as a result. With persistent and consistent riding, Troy will eventually learn to correct his posture himself.

CASE HISTORY… My horse sets her jaw and neck

1 Without taking a step, you can learn a lot about the type of problem you might be about to encounter on a particular horse. Even at halt, Bailey's resistance to the bit shows clearly as tightness and rigidity through her jaw and neck – she's not responding to the reasonable amount of pressure I'm exerting and is almost 'holding' the bit between clenched teeth. In addition it is clear her attention is elsewhere: note her ears giving me the 'V'-sign! All this tells me immediately that Bailey is not attuned to the concept of pressure and release and needs work on the halter and rope circling before anything else (see pp.64–65, where she is taught these lessons).

2 I try another very simple experiment, which confirms Bailey's total ignorance of the concept of pressure. She is a relatively experienced mare yet to turn her head I literally have to drag it as she shuts her eyes and does her best to pretend she is elsewhere. To break this resistance, I'm going to have to think of something new to stimulate her, as pulling or pinning her down with my hands just isn't the answer. She's heard it all before and has become expert at ignoring it.

5 The next step is to repeat the exercise on the move, in walk. With the change in circumstances, Bailey slips back into her old ways, so I slip back into mine! When she raises her head, I raise my hands.

6 The penny drops that the same rules apply in walk – she lowers her head to find the comfort zone that she knows is there from her experiences at halt. This work takes a lot of patience and persistence, but you'll be surprised how quickly the horse will respond if you are absolutely consistent in your correction. Asking for exaggerated bend can also help break the resistance without a fight and guide her into a position that she will come to realize is more comfortable, but don't combine it with shortening the rein.

...steps to relaxation

4 After some work Bailey begins to remember the pressure-release principle and finds comfort by dropping her head. I immediately lighten my hand to reward her.

3 In addition to plenty of groundwork, which will establish a clear understanding of pressure and release, Bailey needs to do the 'hands up' exercise (see p.98) every time she is ridden. Remember that when you take up a light contact, the horse should not resist. If she does, keep a steady pressure (no fiddling or flexing) to make it obvious to her what you want.

7 Many people think that the moment they encounter any mouth or bit related problems in a horse, the answer is a change of bit. Indeed it might be, but take this step last, not first. Now that I've worked with this mare, I have concluded that she shows such a degree of mental shutdown regarding the bit (probably as a result of years of discomfort) that a new stimulus will help us both. I therefore replace the bit with a hackamore.

8 The results are amazing. This is a great example of how tension in one area – even a relatively small one – can 'jam' the rest of the body and prevent it functioning smoothly and easily. Try running with your jaw clenched or with your arms by your sides. It's tiring, clumsy and very inefficient, even though it's your legs that are running, not the areas you have clenched! Now that her neck and jaw tension have gone, Bailey feels she can use her shoulders and has lifted herself into a light and elegant frame.

CASE HISTORY... My horse bucks and is boisterous

1 In Davy's case, the signs are that this is natural high spirits leading into habitual boisterous and disrespectful behaviour, although, of course, with every example of bucking or misbehaviour of this type, physical pain and saddle fit should be eliminated as a possible factor. Because it's not particularly unseating and at times has been quite an amusing expression of character, Davy's owner, Jane, admits she hasn't taken his bucking seriously and has let Davy perfect his art: from a very bouncy canter, he gets shorter and shorter, puts on the front brakes (left) to tip Jane forward off his back so he is free to let rip with his hind legs (below left).

2 Jane's habit of perching forward and allowing her lower leg to creep too far back (left) probably isn't helping; it may be irritating Davy into reacting and will certainly be decreasing her stability in the saddle, which makes it easier for him to buck.

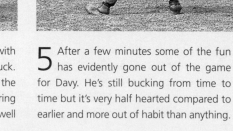

3&4 I get on board and while I'm not doing anything to stop him, Davy realizes with a shock that this passenger is going to make it more difficult for him to buck. I do this by keeping a very secure lower leg and my weight in the saddle, which restricts the freedom of his back and hind legs to get airborne. In addition, every time he bucks, I bring him to a halt, forcing him to put his feet where they belong – back on the ground and well underneath him (centre).

5 After a few minutes some of the fun has evidently gone out of the game for Davy. He's still bucking from time to time but it's very half hearted compared to earlier and more out of habit than anything.

...getting four feet on the ground

6 I try a repetition of the sequence that usually produces the effect pictured earlier, where Davy traditionally slams on the brakes in front and kicks out. He's not having the same success at tipping me forward as he does with Jane. My position doesn't budge, so he decides not to bother. You can almost see him thinking about whether it's worth it!

7 Now we can get on with the job of learning together and because Davy has stopped messing around, I can start riding properly and introducing more interesting exercises that will keep him mentally and physically challenged, which is very important for this type of horse.

9 However, by working on it a little bit at a time – here pushing her leg forward in comparison to how she normally has it and sitting down rather than tipping forward – Jane can discourage those bucks in exactly the same way as I did until Davy loses the habit. As you can see, she's got his respect, focus and attention back so she can get on and ride rather than allowing him to take matters into his own hands.

8 Jane regains the saddle and concentrates on keeping that lower leg in place. Compare this to her previous position (2). As we all know, it's very difficult to alter old habits, especially when it's your own horse and you've both adapted perfectly to suit your mutual strengths and weaknesses! Making a change can be a bit like patting your head and rubbing your stomach, and is certainly not easy on a horse that is taking advantage.

Handling problems and solutions

My horse ... is difficult to catch

This is a common downside associated with the greater freedom enjoyed by horses at grass. Long-term, it's a simple matter of teaching the horse that all good things come from people, and that people are always good! Giving him a scratch or a carrot and letting him go again straight away may be the last thing you want to do if you've just spent an hour trying to catch him, but psychologically, it makes more sense than tacking up and making the horse work. I have found with a high percentage of horses that don't want to be caught, there is an issue related to discomfort. They associate being caught with something unpleasant – the tack, the work itself, the rider, whatever. When you are grooming, look for signs of your horse not enjoying it. If he pulls faces when you are grooming around the girth area or when you are doing up the girth, this may not just indicate that he is ticklish: he may actually be sore in that area. His behaviour when ridden might reinforce this, for example if he bucks or dislikes stretching over poles and fences. Once you have eliminated any physical problems, the horse may take a while to learn that the behaviour is no longer necessary.

SOLUTION I don't like to rely on food for catching a horse: there is always that moment when you don't have any, or the horse is full of summer grass and doesn't want to know. This is the time when join-up and the whole process of 'pushing the horse away' can be really useful. And, hard as it is, once you have caught your horse, I really do strongly recommend that you give him a rub and reward and then turn him away, rather than always bringing him in for work.

When I was a child, my pony, Flicka, would occasionally be difficult to catch. One day I lost my temper and started running at him, twirling the headcollar above my head (I was 13 years old and very mad with the pony). Off he went with his tail in the air and his head high, and I thought I'd made matters worse. When I was exhausted with chasing around, I stopped and walked back to the gate, feeling very dejected. All of a sudden I felt Flicka's presence behind me. The next time I went to catch him, I repeated the performance, and again after less time he came to me. I didn't have a clue why he was doing this but it became a ritual for us – almost a game. I thought he liked to play tag.

Of course, frightening your horse by chasing him round the field for a few minutes is not going to help you catch him, and may even make matters worse, unless you are doing it in a structured way as part of the join-up process. You must be prepared to continue until you get a result, by advancing and retreating, using passive body language and approaching on a 45-degree angle without looking the horse in the eye (for more about the techniques of join-up, see my book *Understanding Your Horse*). With a horse that is really difficult to catch, make life easier for yourself by leaving a headcollar on with a short length of rope attached (make sure they can't stand on the rope when they are grazing and that the headcollar will break if snagged on something). Turn him out in a smaller area so that you don't have to run for miles and you can keep him on the move. If he has 10 minutes to graze and rest at the far end of a huge field while you catch up with him, the odds are against you succeeding!

On one of my courses, a student confessed that he had a horse in a very large field and just couldn't get near him, so he decided to try join-up on a quad bike. Off he went, slowly following this horse around the field and keeping him on the move but without frightening him. Whenever the horse looked like he was going to submit, he got off the bike and tried join-up. If the horse went off again, he jumped on the bike and followed him. Eventually he achieved join-up and the horse followed him home!

My horse ... is stressed in the stable

SOLUTION There are several reasons why horses get stressed in stables, the most obvious of which is that they are herd animals and don't like to be confined, so first of all address your stable management. Horses need several hours of freedom to move and forage, in the company of other horses, every day. If your livery yard does not do this then you need to look around for somewhere that does allow horses to be kept in such a way.

Some horses have also learnt that temper tantrums give them a form of control over their owner, even if the owner's reaction is negative. I had one such pony sent to me for retraining. As soon as the owner got up in the morning she had to creep around and not put any lights on, as he went crazy and smashed his stable up if he wasn't fed within about 30 seconds. When he came to my yard, he never really displayed this behaviour. I came to believe that it wasn't about food or stables at all; it was about dominance. He knew he wasn't in charge anymore and that I was the boss. The key was to get the owner involved so she became the new boss and the pony realized he was no longer number one. We did this through the groundwork, and getting his owner to be a bit more assertive with him, quietly taking control of the situation. If you own a horse like this, analyze your whole relationship rather than just the one particular problem; you'll probably come up with quite a few areas where the horse takes control, whether it's when he's being handled, led or ridden.

My horse ... is unsettled by changes

SOLUTION While all horses like their routine, some do become particularly upset and unsettled by change, and they are generally insecure about many things.

We take in youngsters to back and come across many owners who are worried about their young horses and how they will cope with the new environment. Some horses have never been stabled or even travelled before, so it's understandable that their owners are apprehensive. What I have found is that after the owner has gone home and the youngsters are handled in a quiet but reassuring way, they soon settle in. Horses feed off the emotions of others, it's how they survive in a herd. If one horse looks alert, they all do. In the wild, there are not many horses that would refuse to gallop off with the herd, instead staying put to see if it really is a lion over there! It's the same at a show or other outing away from home. Providing he is physically comfortable, an unsettled horse probably has a nervous or tense rider, and he's wondering what's going to happen to him. Of course, there is always the situation where a horse has had a bad experience, but if through the groundwork you have built up a relationship where he looks to you for reassurance then that should ease as the trust grows.

I know that my nerves affect my horse, Pelo. At home he is absolutely fine, but when we take him away to demos or showjumping, my blood is up and he is exactly the same. He knows we are going to be doing something different. In fact, he has come to really enjoy performing, a far cry from what he was like when I bought him. In those days, he used to be fine until something changed or a tractor drove past, then he turned into an emotional mess. Now his confidence and trust is restored, he is a star and loves to show off in front of crowds.

Postscript

For me there are going to be a few changes over the next few years. Firstly, I am going to cut back on the number of days that I go out to people's homes and yards. Although it's what I love to do I also have to spend more time at home with my three boys, James, William and Jack.

Secondly, I would like to spend more time improving myself – especially in my ridden work. I would like to study Classical riding and try to work out how I can marry this with my own training philosophies.

Also if I improve my seat and balance it should improve all areas – especially my jumping and I would love to spend time with someone like Tim Stockdale.

I have also been invited to spend some time with the 'Devil's Horsemen', the stunt-team based in Milton Keynes which I am very much looking forward to.

Lastly, I would like to be able to spend some time with Nosey (King's Copy) the stallion given to me by Cathy Hedges. He has really changed in the last 12 months and although I have now had him for 5 years he gives me the feeling that he will now let me ride him – all be it bareback.It's my dream to be able to do some dressage to music, bareback and bridleless. Watch out for demonstrations in 2004.

I would also like to take this opportunity to thank everyone that has supported me over the years – believe it or not it was never my intention to be a well-know horseman – just a good one.

All the equipment I use can be obtained from:
Equestrian Merchandise Ltd
14 Woodyard Close, Brigstock
Northampton NN14 3LZ, UK
Tel: 01536 373049

To arrange a visit or demonstration contact Nikki at Equestrian Services Ltd. Tel: 01799 542738

To contact Greg Wood, Equine Dentist tel: 02380 692671

Finally, I would like to dedicate this book to Andy Andrews, who died in October last year. He is sadly missed, not just by me but by the many horses he treated.

Index